My Life Beyond
DIABETES

A Mayo Clinic patient story
by Hey Gee and Wolf Queen

Foreword

When I was little, I didn't feel good and I had to go to the hospital. We found out that I had type 1 diabetes. It means my body doesn't make **insulin** to help me process sugar. At first, it was scary. There were lots of people there telling me all kinds of different things that I need to do for the rest of my life. My mom is a nurse, so she already knew about diabetes, but my dad and I didn't.

We stayed there for a few days and learned all about diabetes and how to manage it. The good part was that I started to feel better because I was getting the **insulin** that I needed. The bad part was I had to get lots of shots and prick my finger a bunch to check my **blood sugar.** At first this was kind of hard to do, and I didn't really like it. I still don't love getting shots and pricking my finger, but at least it's easier now, and when people see me do it, they always say how brave and strong I am.

People always ask me what I can and can't do because of my diabetes. They also ask if I can eat candy, ice cream and cake. At first, I wondered about these things too. Now I know that I can do anything other kids do — I just have to plan ahead. I also know more about food and nutrition than most kids my age. I think that will make me a healthier person for my whole life.

I hope everyone reading this book knows that kids with diabetes can do anything other kids can do — even go on an adventure!

Wolf Queen

"

DIABETES SHOULD NEVER STOP YOU FROM DOING ANYTHING YOU CAN DREAM OF

"

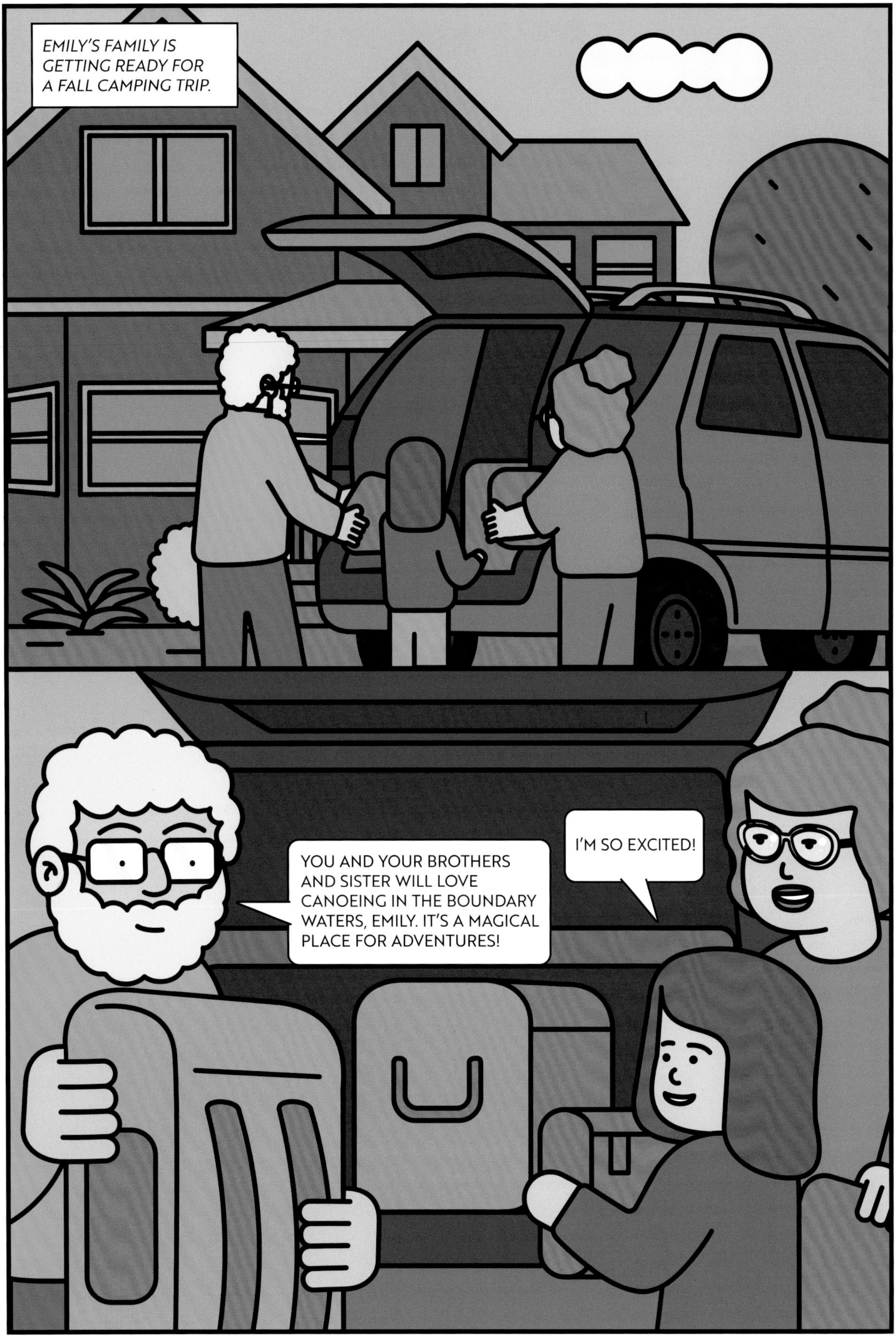
EMILY'S FAMILY IS GETTING READY FOR A FALL CAMPING TRIP.
YOU AND YOUR BROTHERS AND SISTER WILL LOVE CANOEING IN THE BOUNDARY WATERS, EMILY. IT'S A MAGICAL PLACE FOR ADVENTURES!
I'M SO EXCITED!

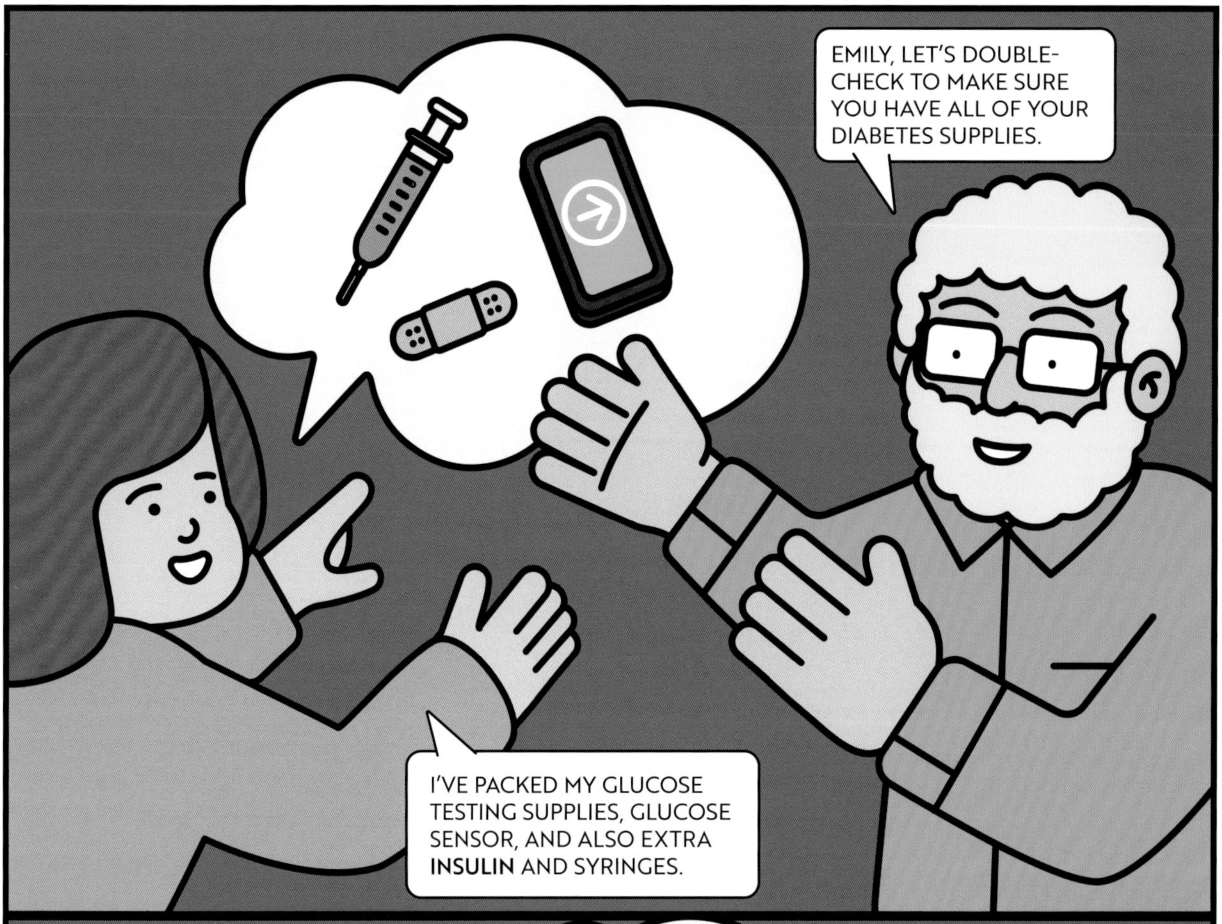
EMILY, LET'S DOUBLE-CHECK TO MAKE SURE YOU HAVE ALL OF YOUR DIABETES SUPPLIES.
I'VE PACKED MY GLUCOSE TESTING SUPPLIES, GLUCOSE SENSOR, AND ALSO EXTRA **INSULIN** AND SYRINGES.

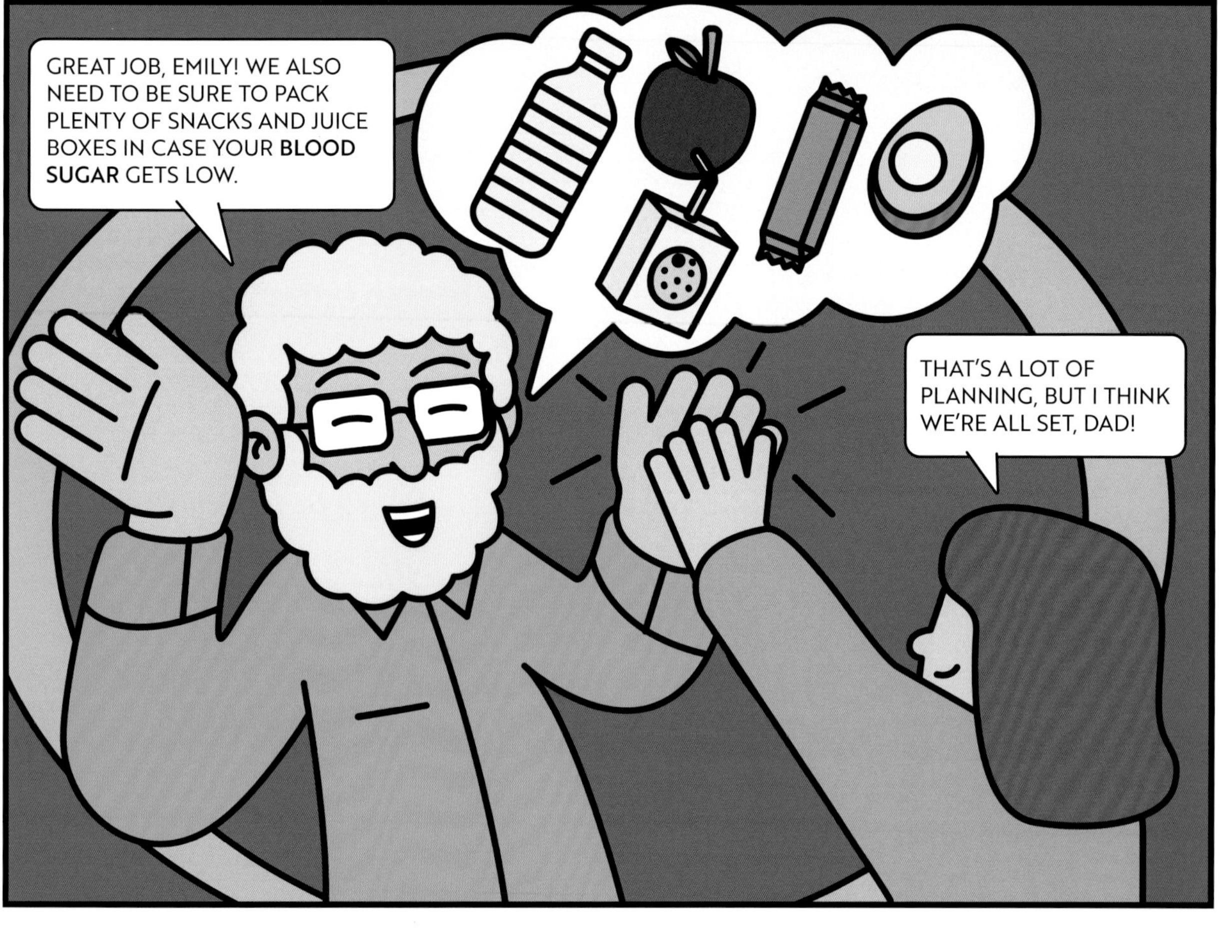
GREAT JOB, EMILY! WE ALSO NEED TO BE SURE TO PACK PLENTY OF SNACKS AND JUICE BOXES IN CASE YOUR **BLOOD SUGAR** GETS LOW.
THAT'S A LOT OF PLANNING, BUT I THINK WE'RE ALL SET, DAD!

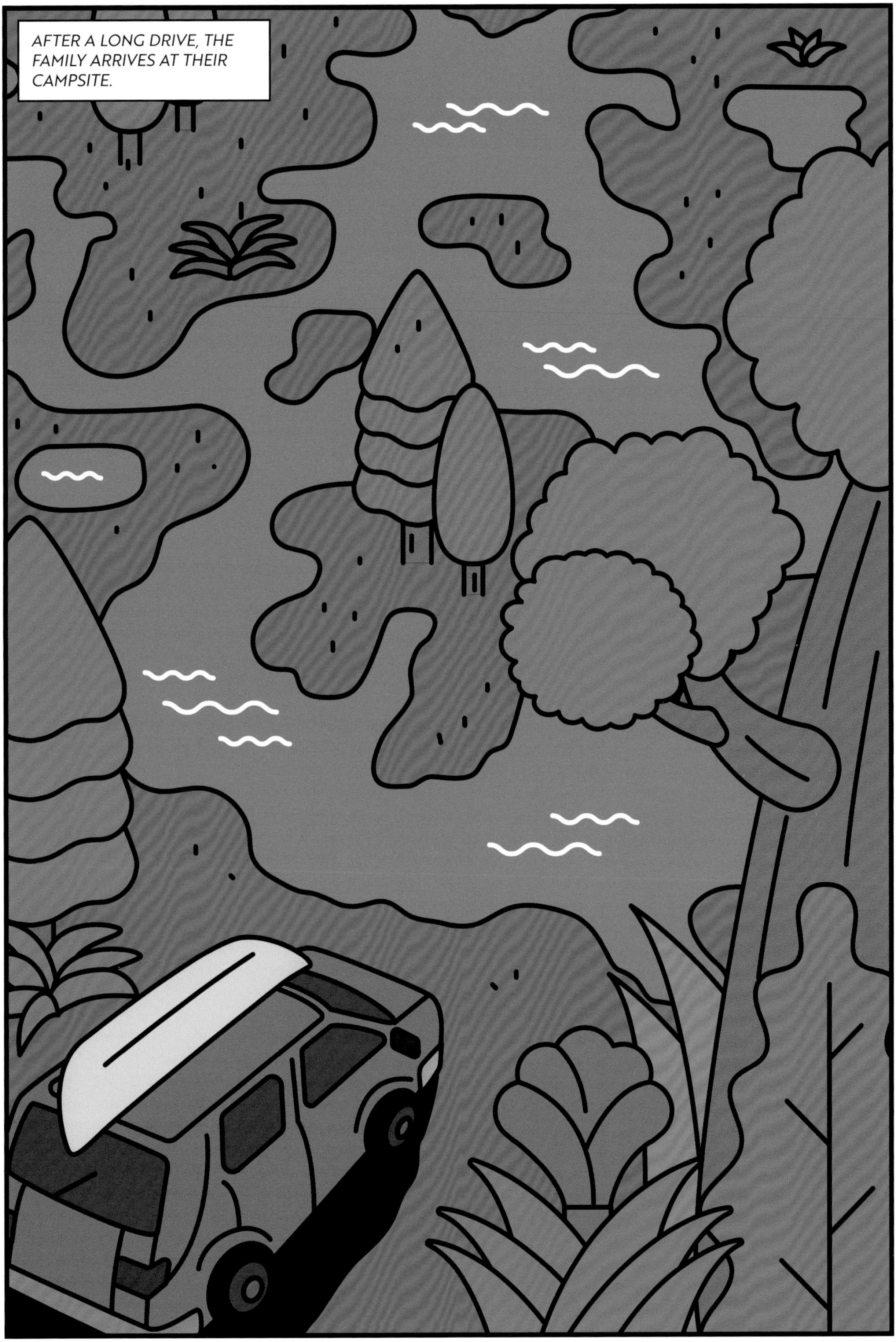
AFTER A LONG DRIVE, THE FAMILY ARRIVES AT THEIR CAMPSITE.

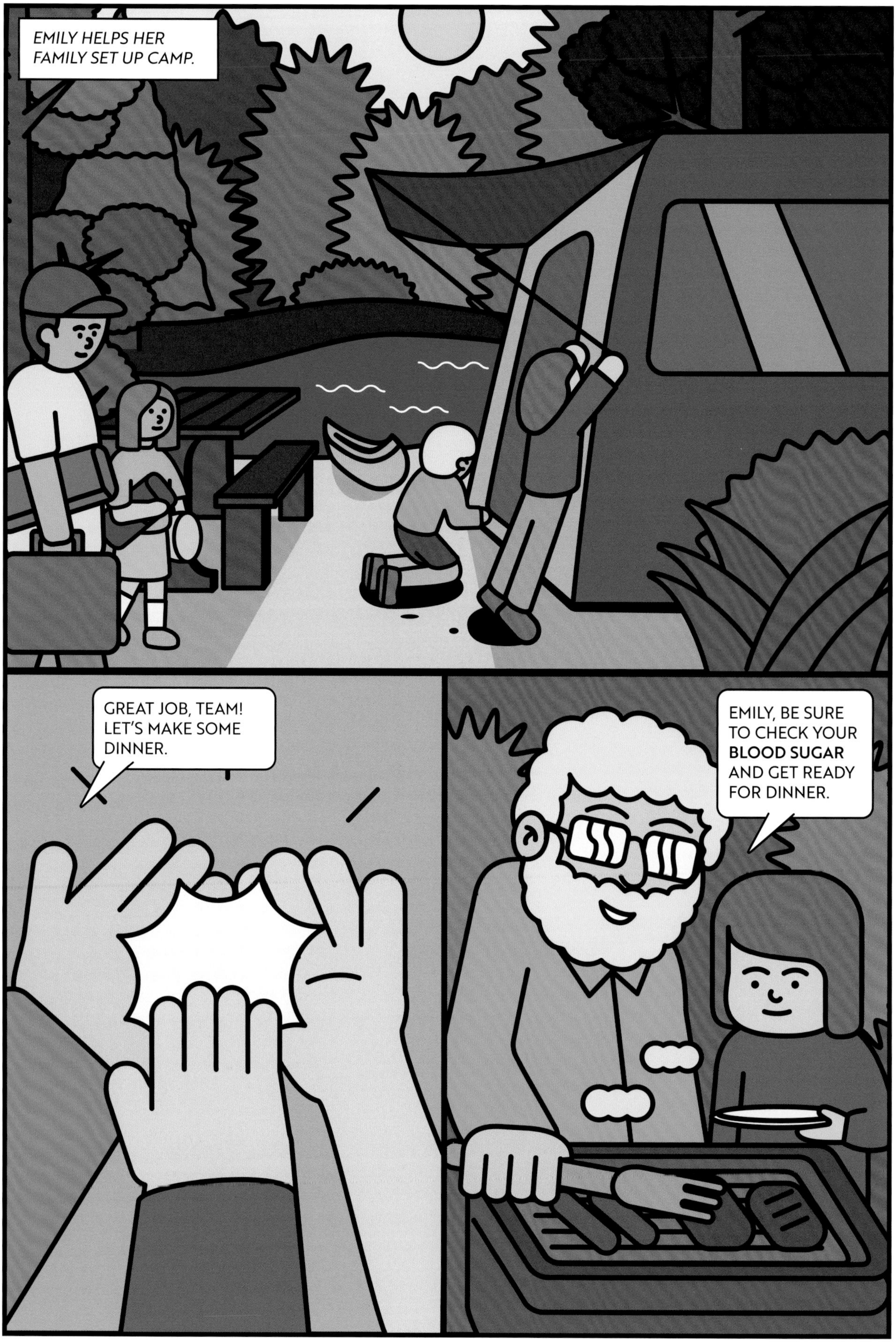
EMILY HELPS HER FAMILY SET UP CAMP.
GREAT JOB, TEAM! LET'S MAKE SOME DINNER.
EMILY, BE SURE TO CHECK YOUR **BLOOD SUGAR** AND GET READY FOR DINNER.

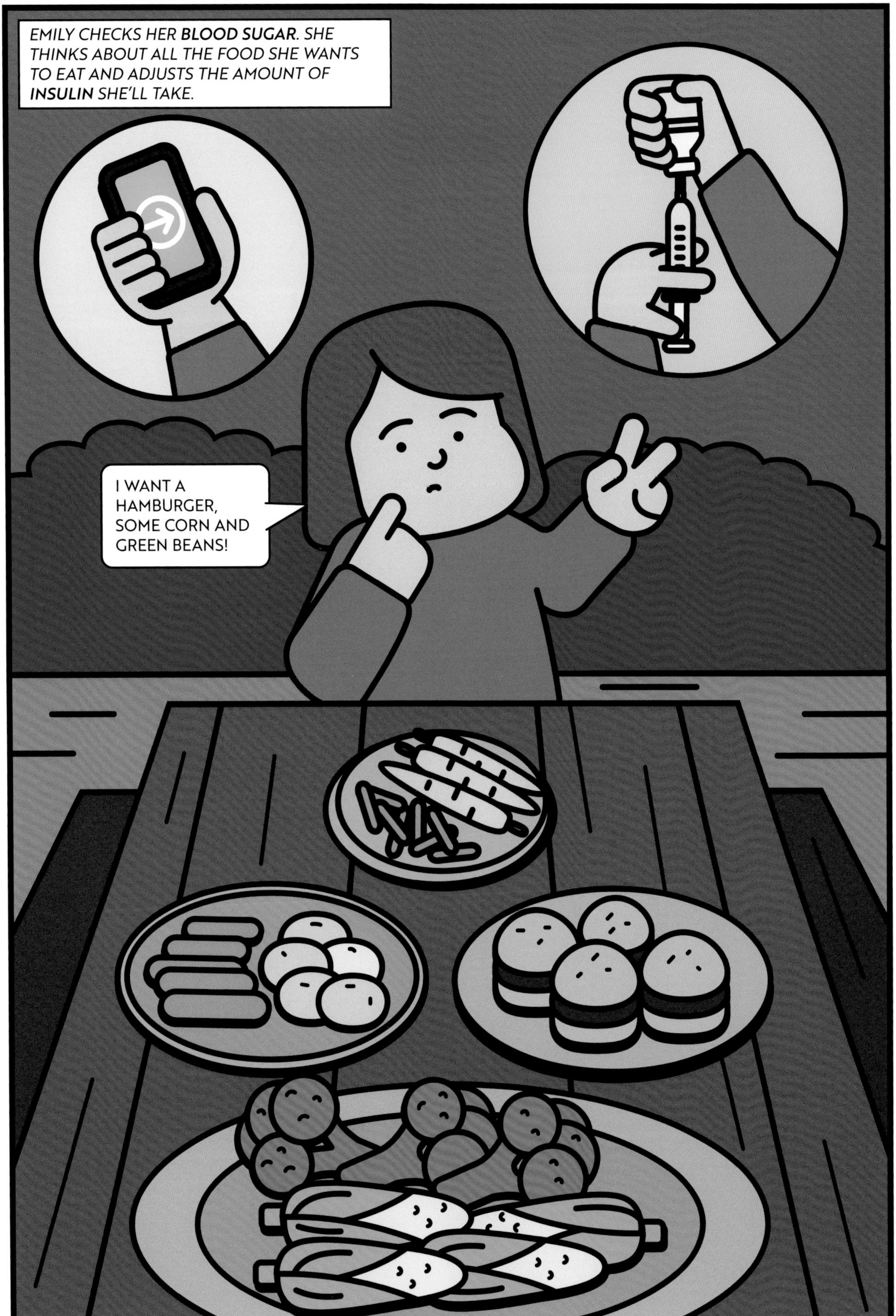
EMILY CHECKS HER **BLOOD SUGAR**. SHE THINKS ABOUT ALL THE FOOD SHE WANTS TO EAT AND ADJUSTS THE AMOUNT OF **INSULIN** SHE'LL TAKE.
I WANT A HAMBURGER, SOME CORN AND GREEN BEANS!

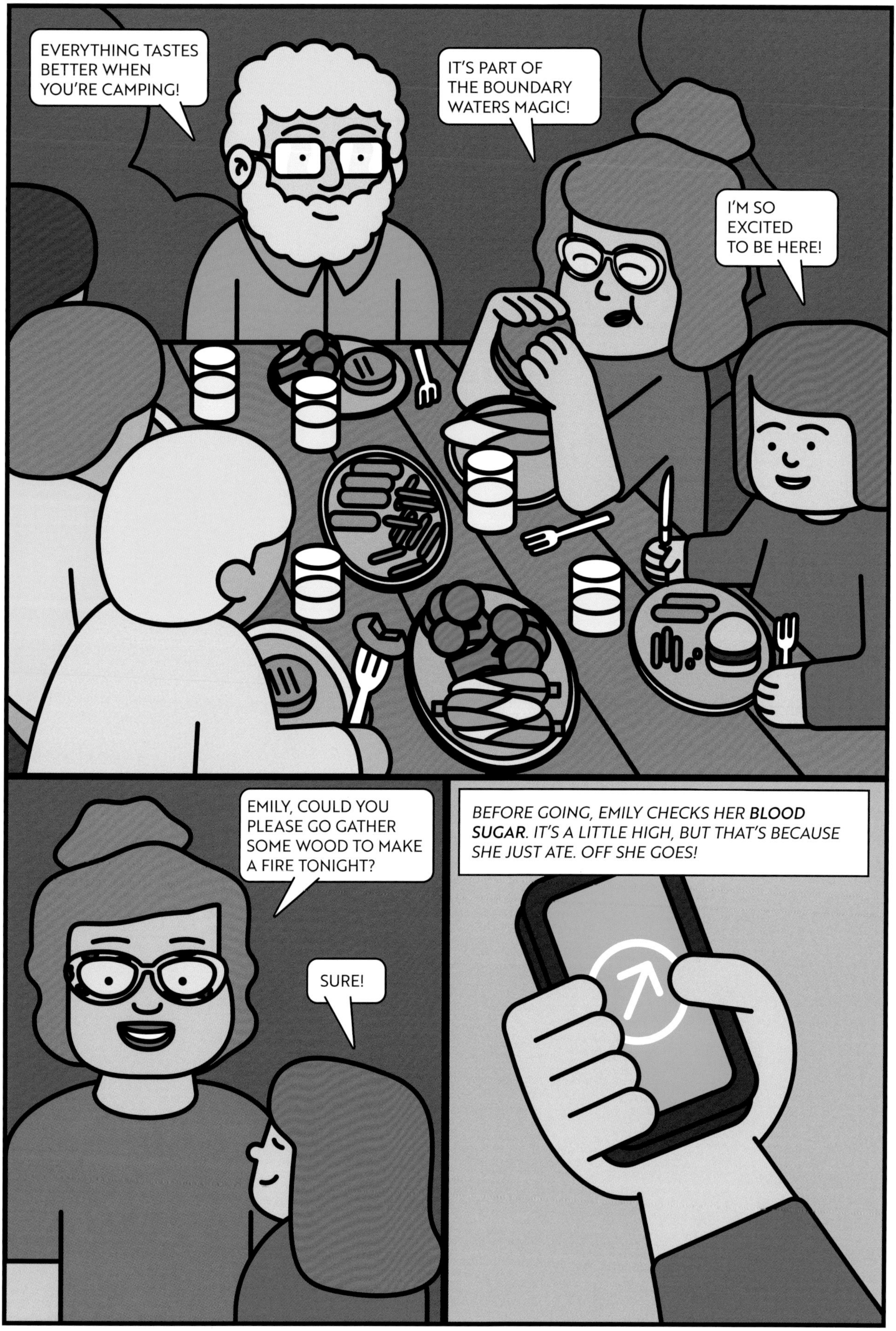
EVERYTHING TASTES BETTER WHEN YOU'RE CAMPING!
IT'S PART OF THE BOUNDARY WATERS MAGIC!
I'M SO EXCITED TO BE HERE!
EMILY, COULD YOU PLEASE GO GATHER SOME WOOD TO MAKE A FIRE TONIGHT?
SURE!
*BEFORE GOING, EMILY CHECKS HER **BLOOD SUGAR**. IT'S A LITTLE HIGH, BUT THAT'S BECAUSE SHE JUST ATE. OFF SHE GOES!*

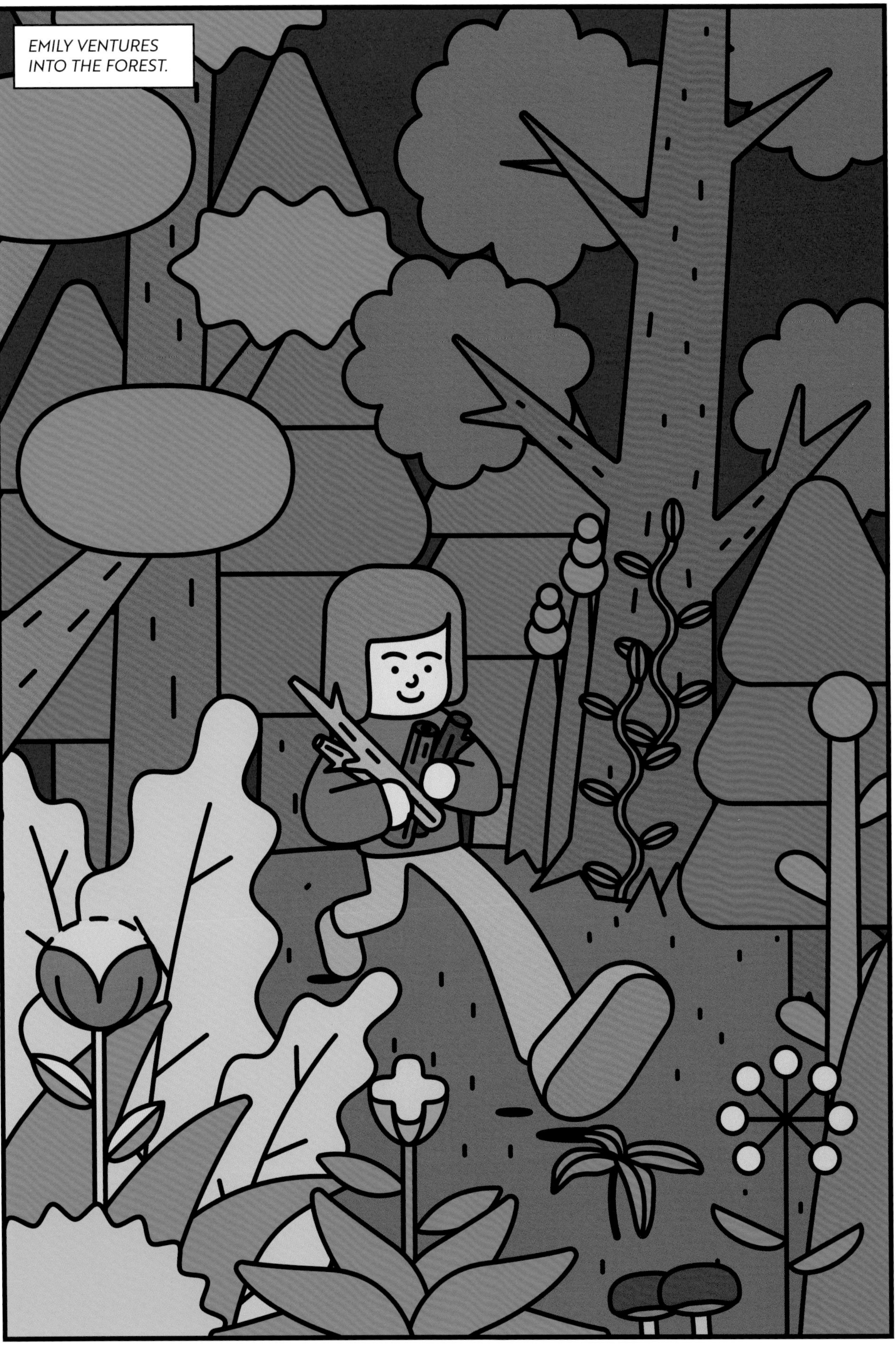
EMILY VENTURES INTO THE FOREST.

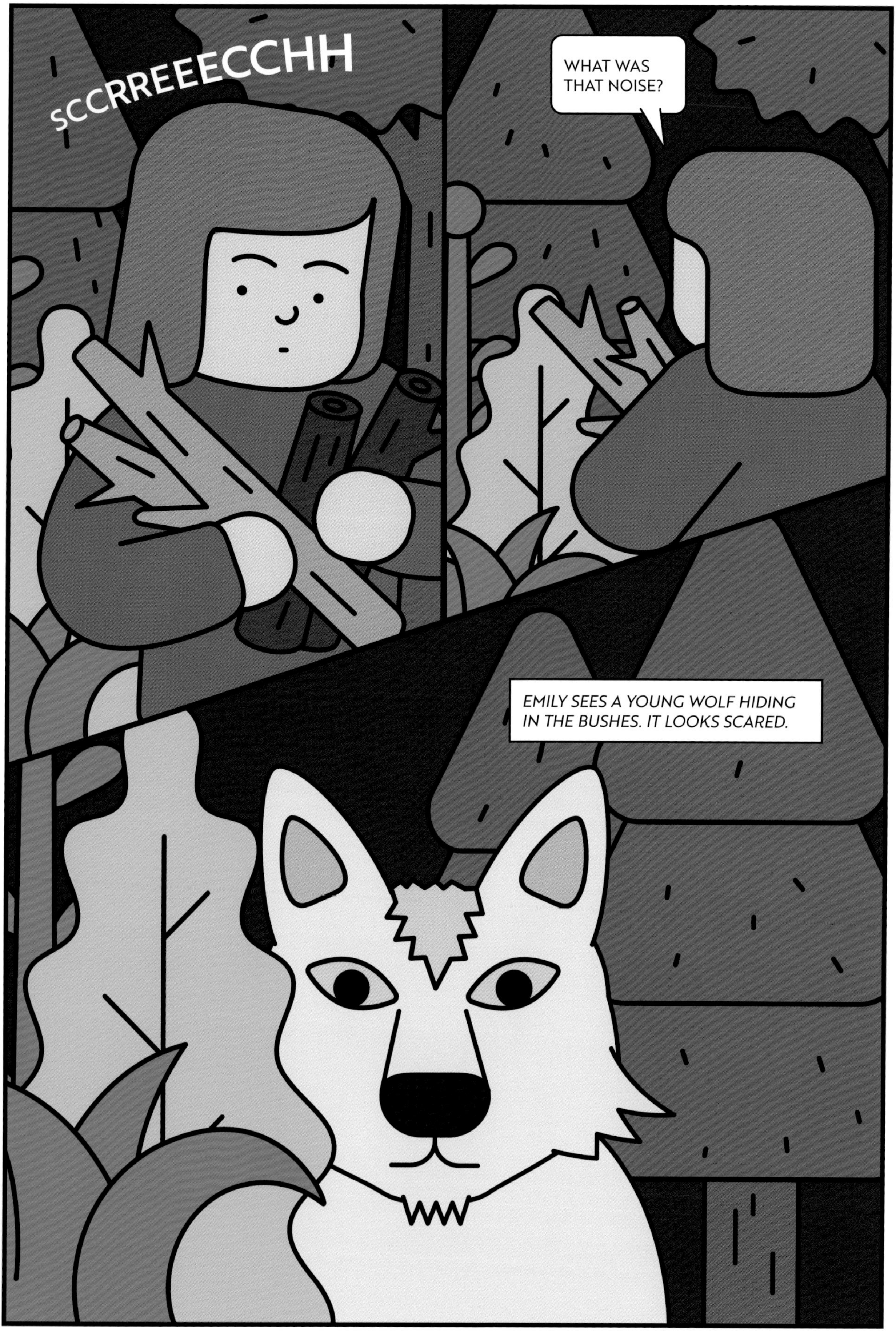
SCCRREEEECCHH
WHAT WAS THAT NOISE?
EMILY SEES A YOUNG WOLF HIDING IN THE BUSHES. IT LOOKS SCARED.

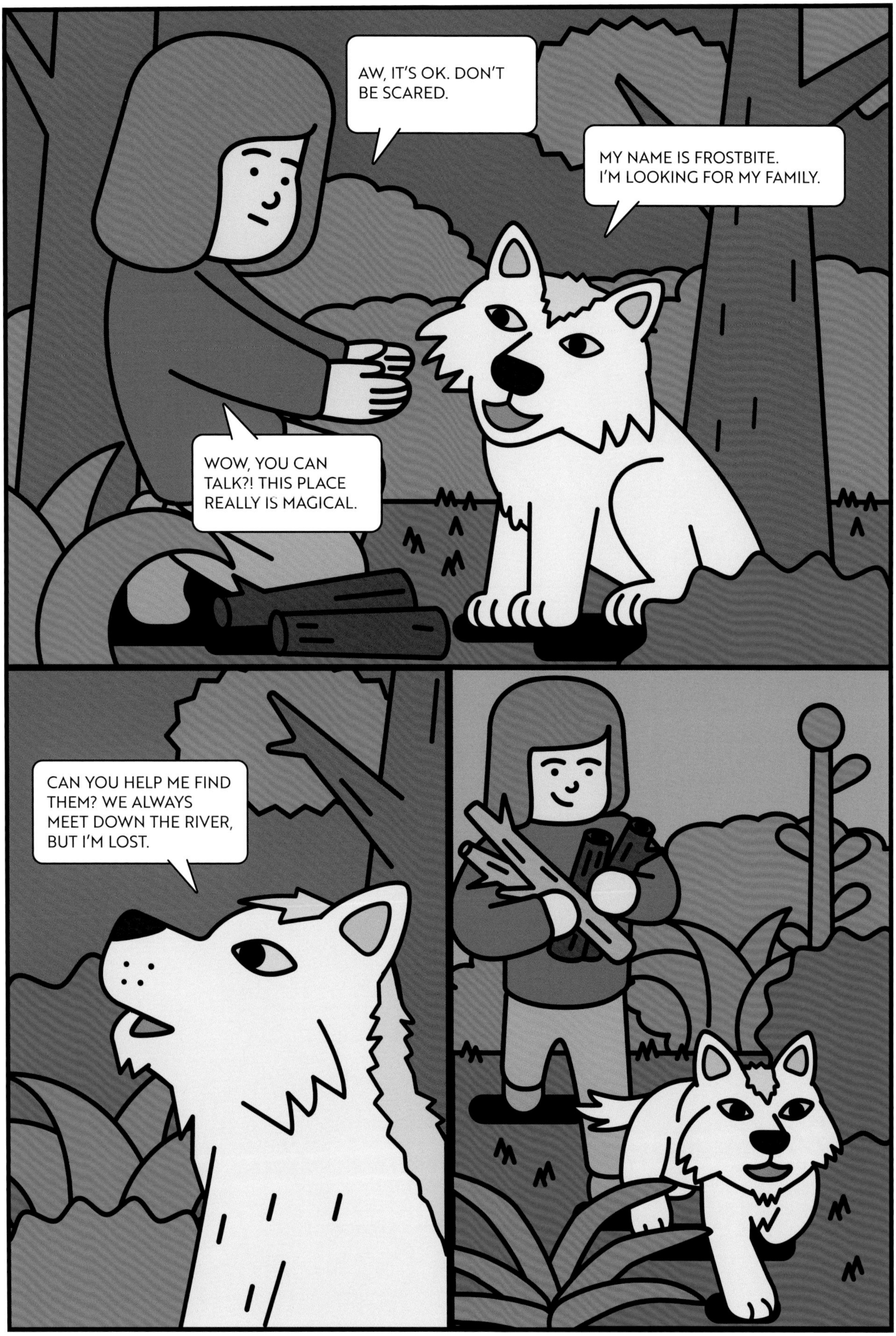
AW, IT'S OK. DON'T BE SCARED.
MY NAME IS FROSTBITE. I'M LOOKING FOR MY FAMILY.
WOW, YOU CAN TALK?! THIS PLACE REALLY IS MAGICAL.
CAN YOU HELP ME FIND THEM? WE ALWAYS MEET DOWN THE RIVER, BUT I'M LOST.

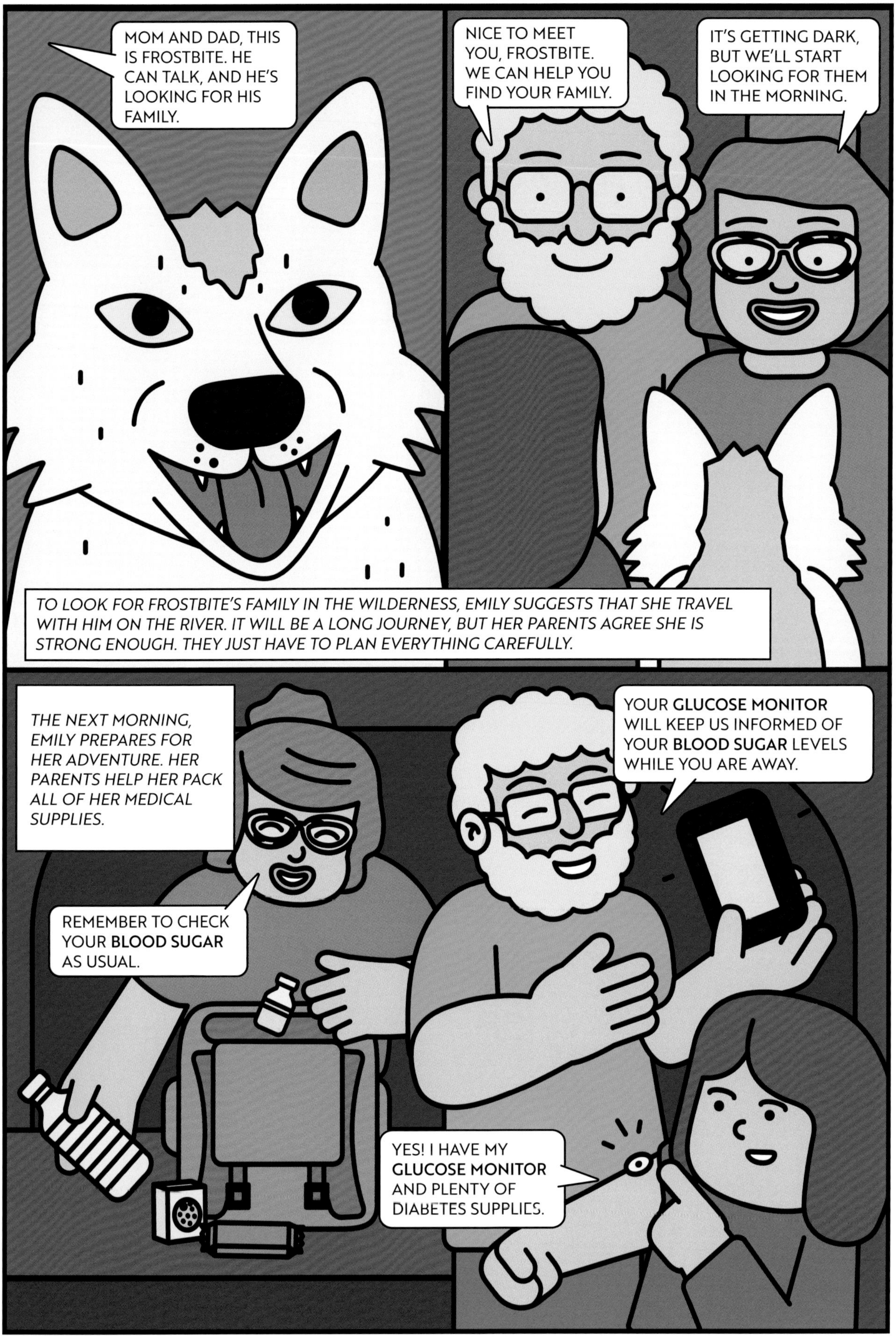
MOM AND DAD, THIS IS FROSTBITE. HE CAN TALK, AND HE'S LOOKING FOR HIS FAMILY.
NICE TO MEET YOU, FROSTBITE. WE CAN HELP YOU FIND YOUR FAMILY.
IT'S GETTING DARK, BUT WE'LL START LOOKING FOR THEM IN THE MORNING.
TO LOOK FOR FROSTBITE'S FAMILY IN THE WILDERNESS, EMILY SUGGESTS THAT SHE TRAVEL WITH HIM ON THE RIVER. IT WILL BE A LONG JOURNEY, BUT HER PARENTS AGREE SHE IS STRONG ENOUGH. THEY JUST HAVE TO PLAN EVERYTHING CAREFULLY.
THE NEXT MORNING, EMILY PREPARES FOR HER ADVENTURE. HER PARENTS HELP HER PACK ALL OF HER MEDICAL SUPPLIES.
YOUR **GLUCOSE MONITOR** WILL KEEP US INFORMED OF YOUR **BLOOD SUGAR** LEVELS WHILE YOU ARE AWAY.
REMEMBER TO CHECK YOUR **BLOOD SUGAR** AS USUAL.
YES! I HAVE MY **GLUCOSE MONITOR** AND PLENTY OF DIABETES SUPPLIES.

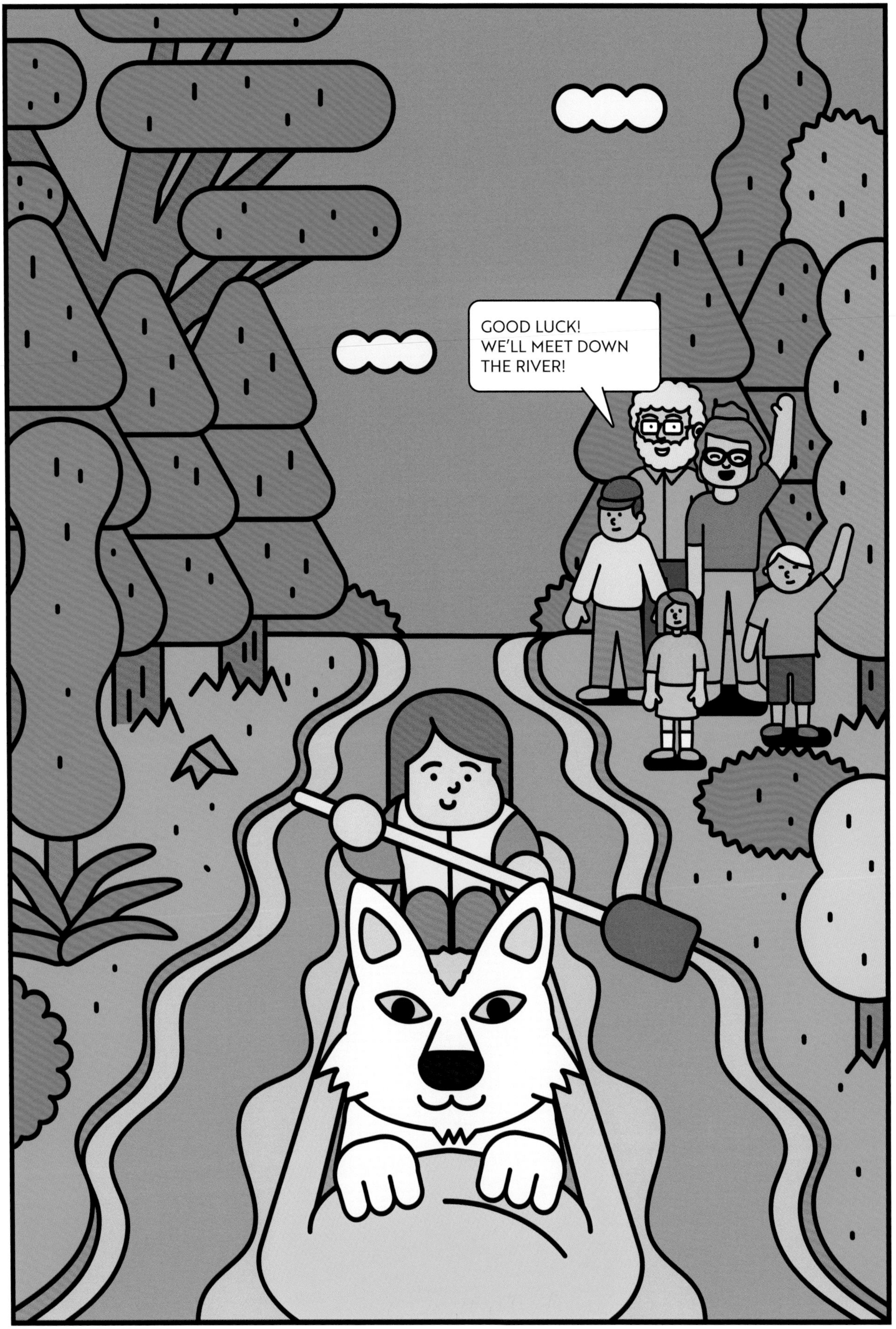
GOOD LUCK! WE'LL MEET DOWN THE RIVER!

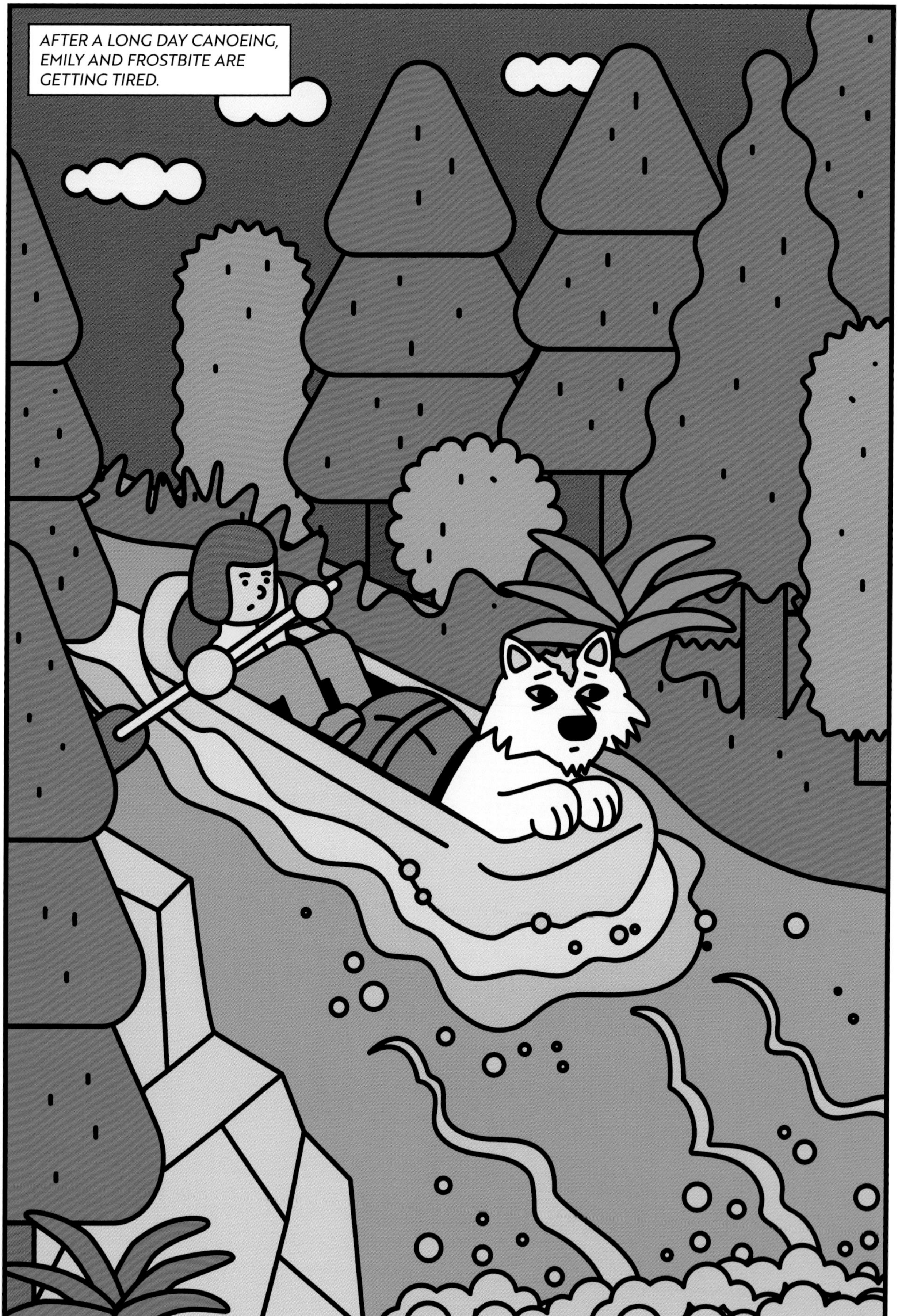
AFTER A LONG DAY CANOEING, EMILY AND FROSTBITE ARE GETTING TIRED.

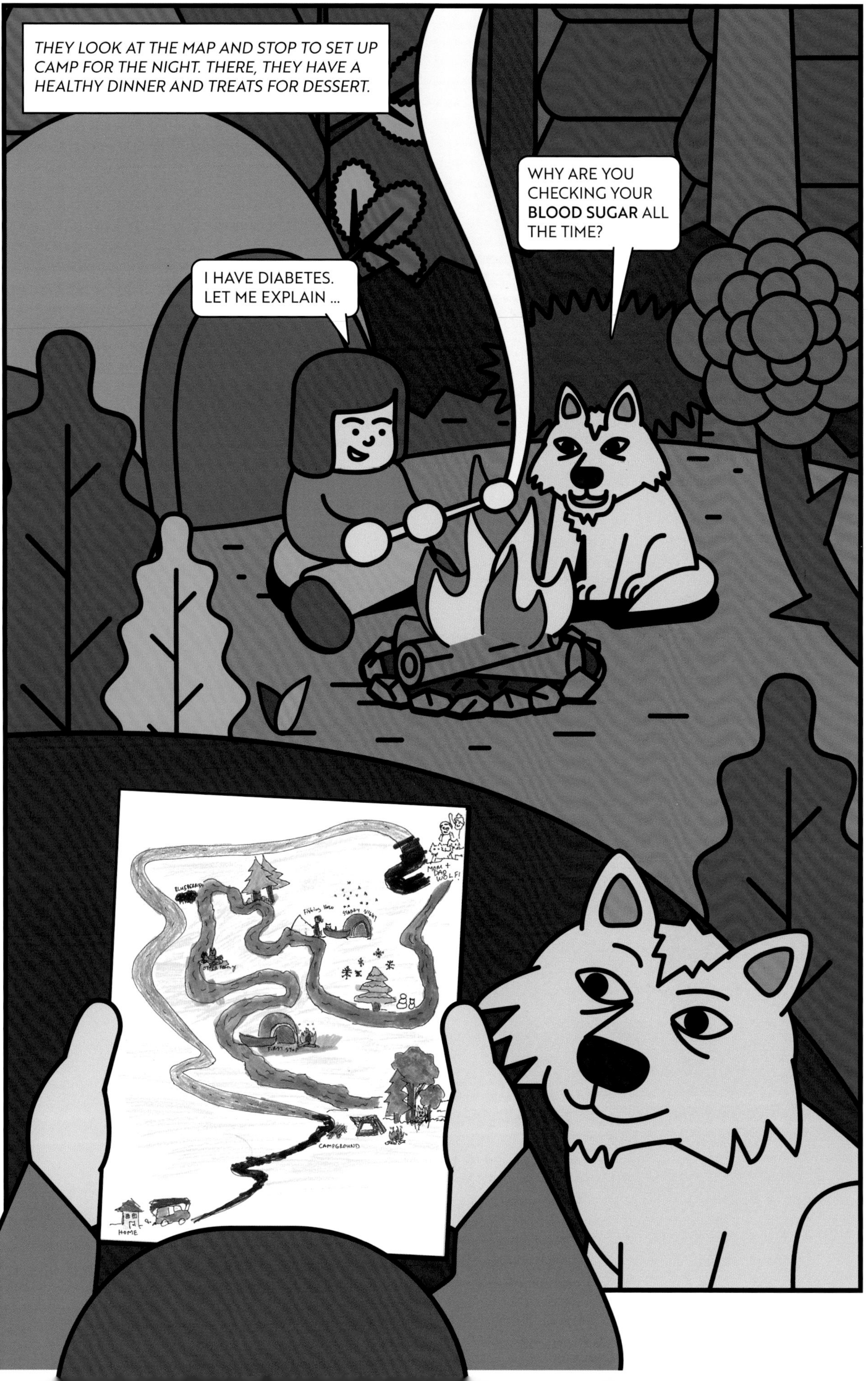

THEY LOOK AT THE MAP AND STOP TO SET UP CAMP FOR THE NIGHT. THERE, THEY HAVE A HEALTHY DINNER AND TREATS FOR DESSERT.
WHY ARE YOU CHECKING YOUR **BLOOD SUGAR** ALL THE TIME?
I HAVE DIABETES. LET ME EXPLAIN ...
FIRST STOP
CAMPGROUND
HOME

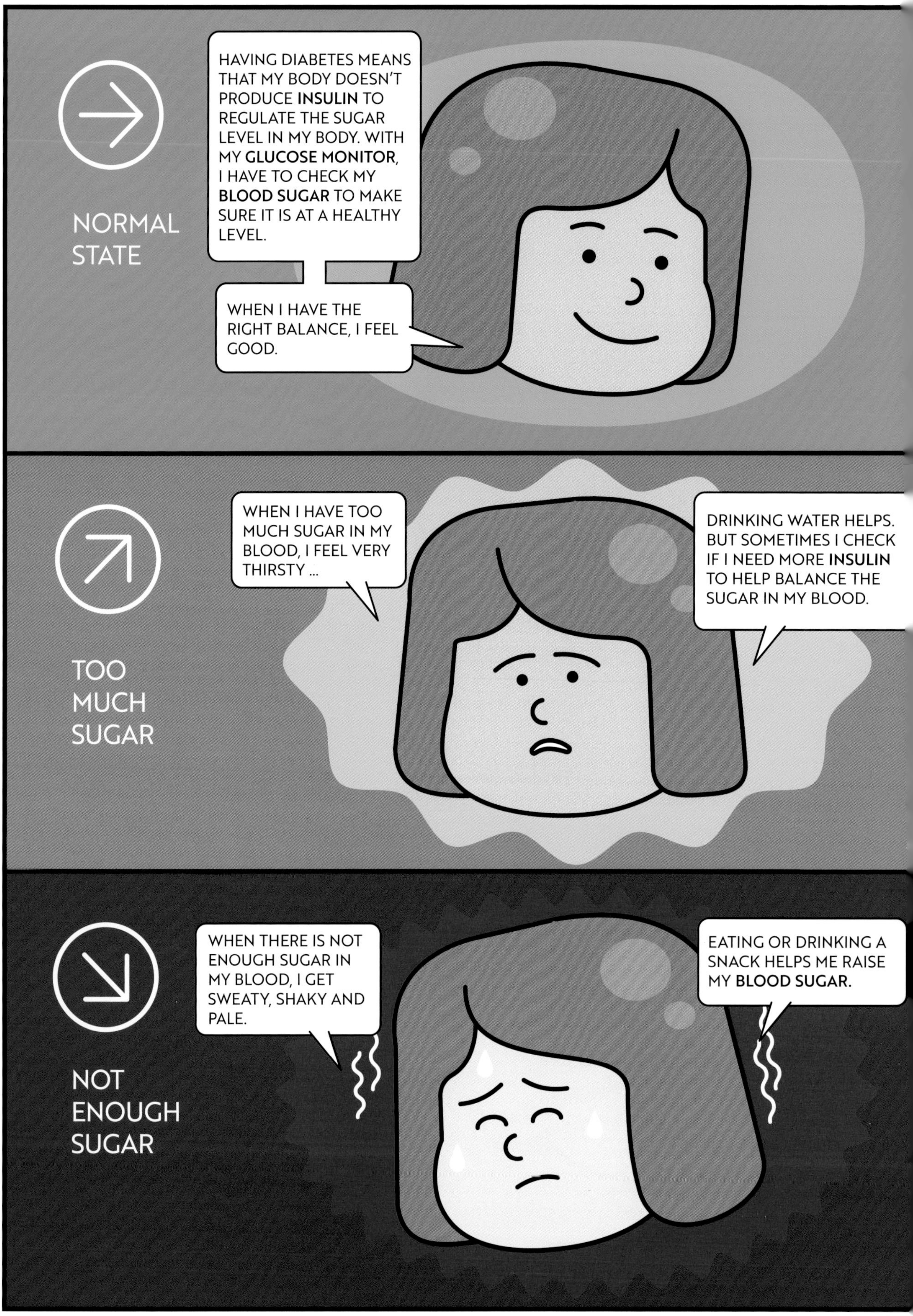
NORMAL STATE
HAVING DIABETES MEANS THAT MY BODY DOESN'T PRODUCE **INSULIN** TO REGULATE THE SUGAR LEVEL IN MY BODY. WITH MY **GLUCOSE MONITOR**, I HAVE TO CHECK MY **BLOOD SUGAR** TO MAKE SURE IT IS AT A HEALTHY LEVEL.
WHEN I HAVE THE RIGHT BALANCE, I FEEL GOOD.
TOO MUCH SUGAR
WHEN I HAVE TOO MUCH SUGAR IN MY BLOOD, I FEEL VERY THIRSTY ...
DRINKING WATER HELPS. BUT SOMETIMES I CHECK IF I NEED MORE **INSULIN** TO HELP BALANCE THE SUGAR IN MY BLOOD.
NOT ENOUGH SUGAR
WHEN THERE IS NOT ENOUGH SUGAR IN MY BLOOD, I GET SWEATY, SHAKY AND PALE.
EATING OR DRINKING A SNACK HELPS ME RAISE MY **BLOOD SUGAR.**

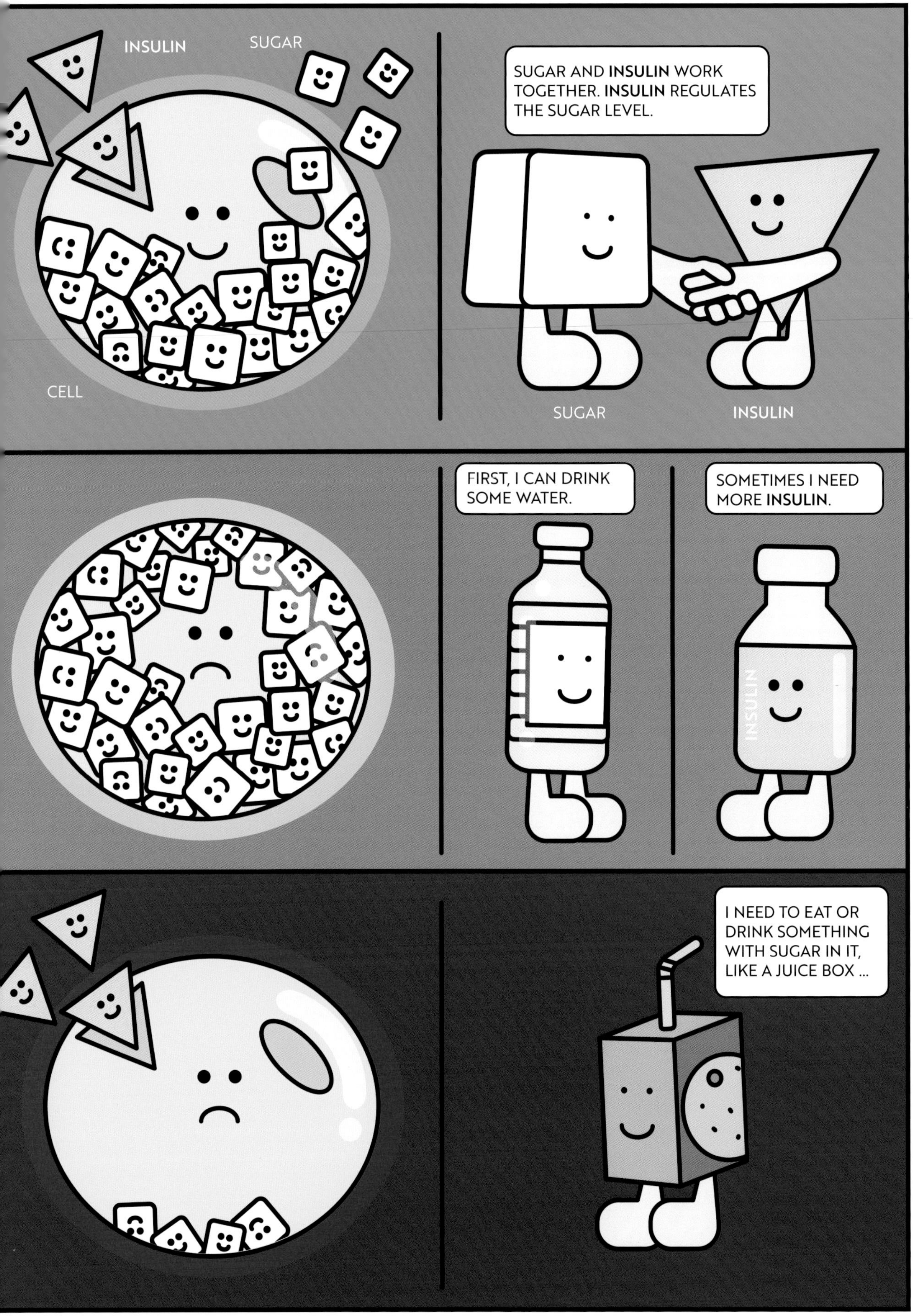
INSULIN
SUGAR
CELL
SUGAR AND INSULIN WORK TOGETHER. INSULIN REGULATES THE SUGAR LEVEL.
SUGAR
INSULIN
FIRST, I CAN DRINK SOME WATER.
SOMETIMES I NEED MORE INSULIN.
INSULIN
I NEED TO EAT OR DRINK SOMETHING WITH SUGAR IN IT, LIKE A JUICE BOX ...

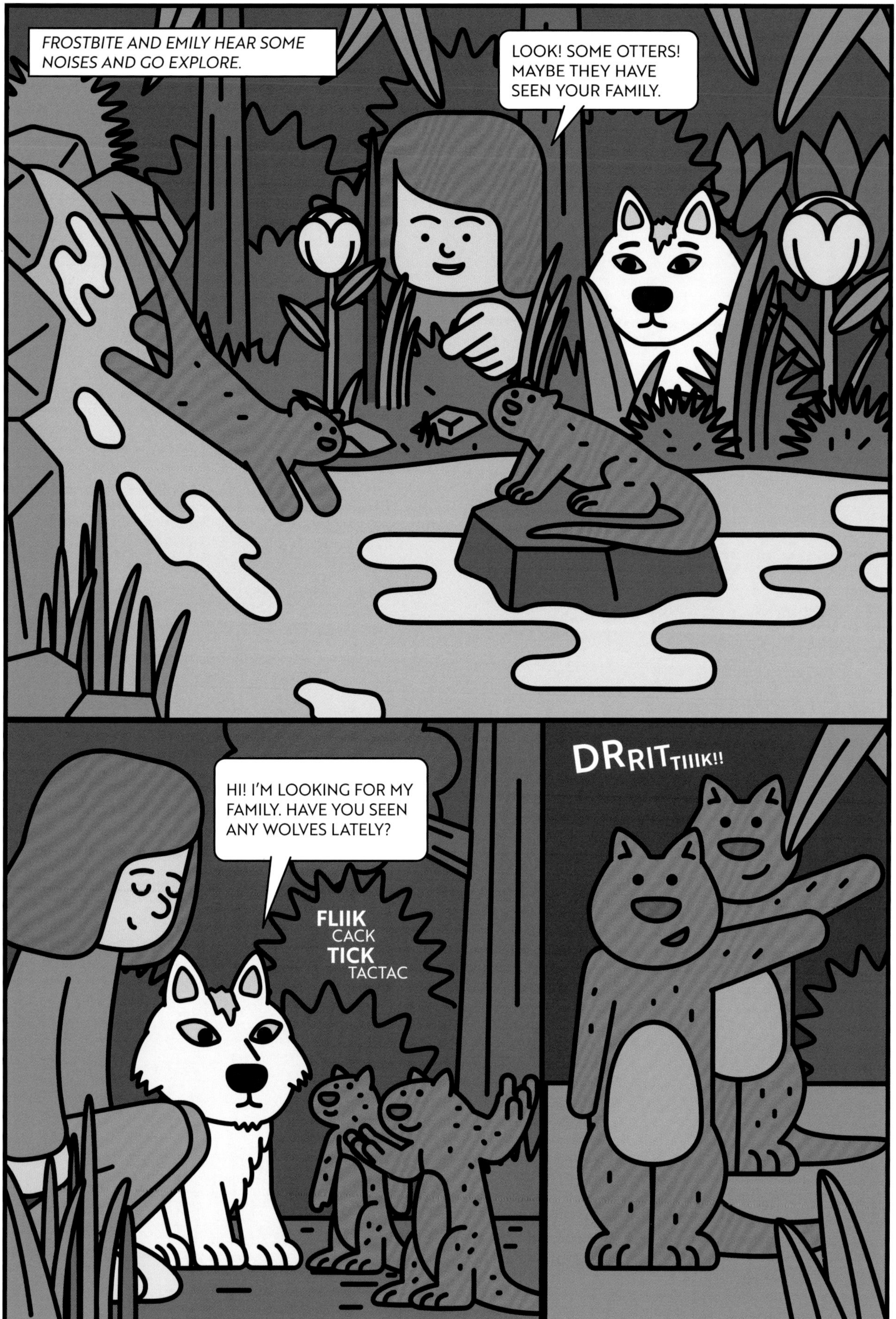
FROSTBITE AND EMILY HEAR SOME NOISES AND GO EXPLORE.
LOOK! SOME OTTERS! MAYBE THEY HAVE SEEN YOUR FAMILY.
HI! I'M LOOKING FOR MY FAMILY. HAVE YOU SEEN ANY WOLVES LATELY?
FLIIK CACK TICK TACTAC
DRRITTIIIK!!

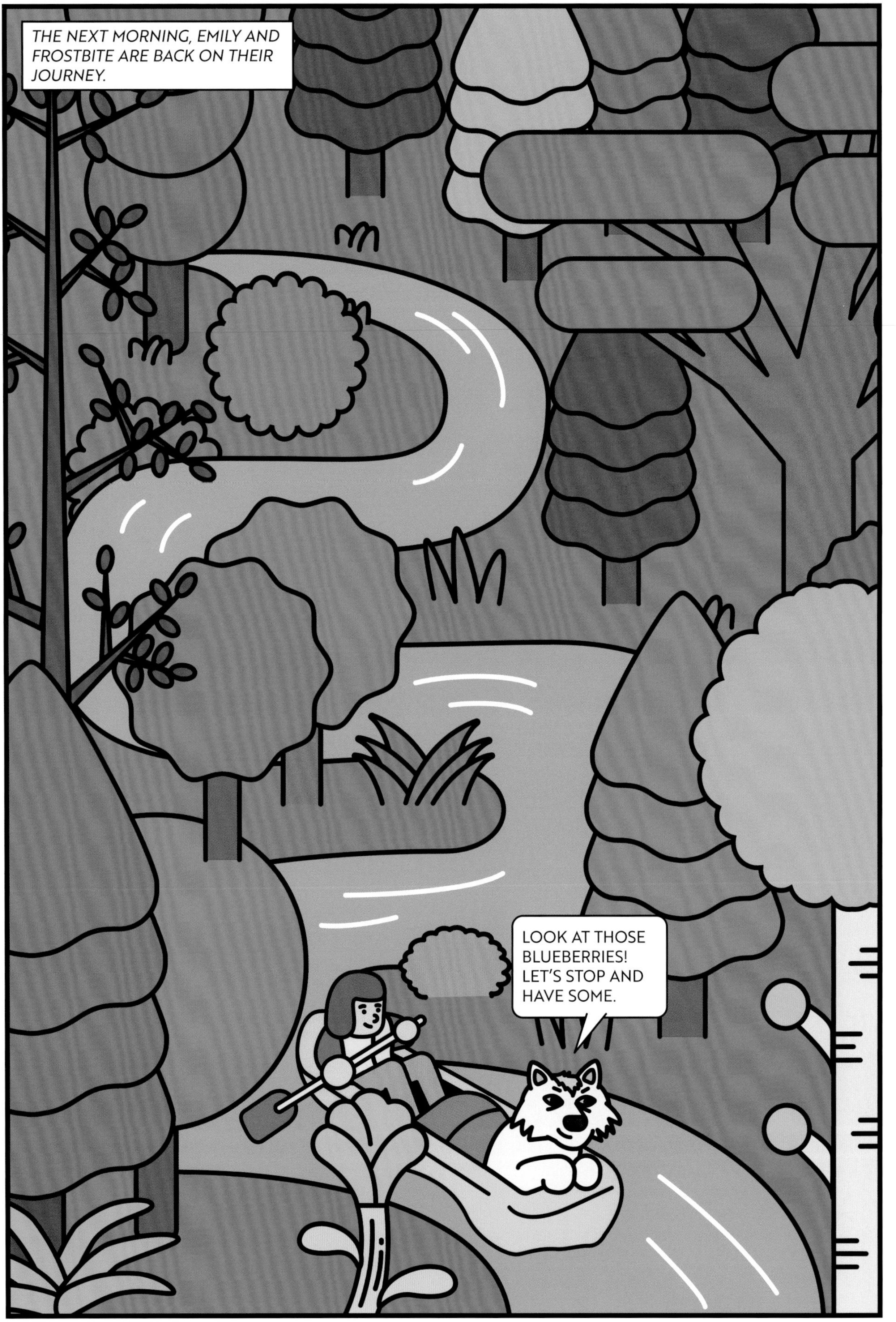
THE NEXT MORNING, EMILY AND FROSTBITE ARE BACK ON THEIR JOURNEY.
LOOK AT THOSE BLUEBERRIES! LET'S STOP AND HAVE SOME.

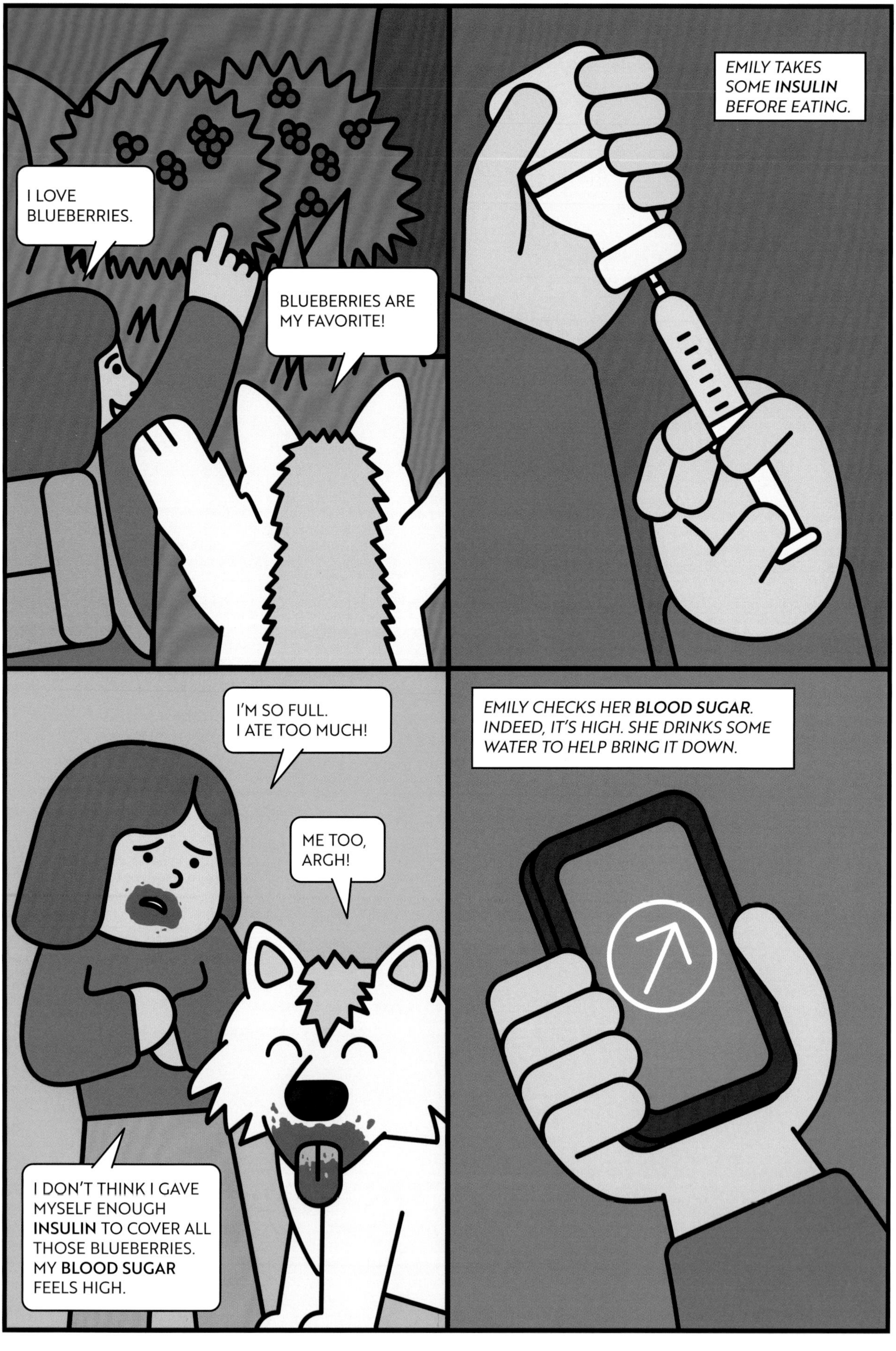
I LOVE BLUEBERRIES.
BLUEBERRIES ARE MY FAVORITE!
EMILY TAKES SOME **INSULIN** BEFORE EATING.
I'M SO FULL. I ATE TOO MUCH!
ME TOO, ARGH!
I DON'T THINK I GAVE MYSELF ENOUGH **INSULIN** TO COVER ALL THOSE BLUEBERRIES. MY **BLOOD SUGAR** FEELS HIGH.
EMILY CHECKS HER **BLOOD SUGAR**. INDEED, IT'S HIGH. SHE DRINKS SOME WATER TO HELP BRING IT DOWN.

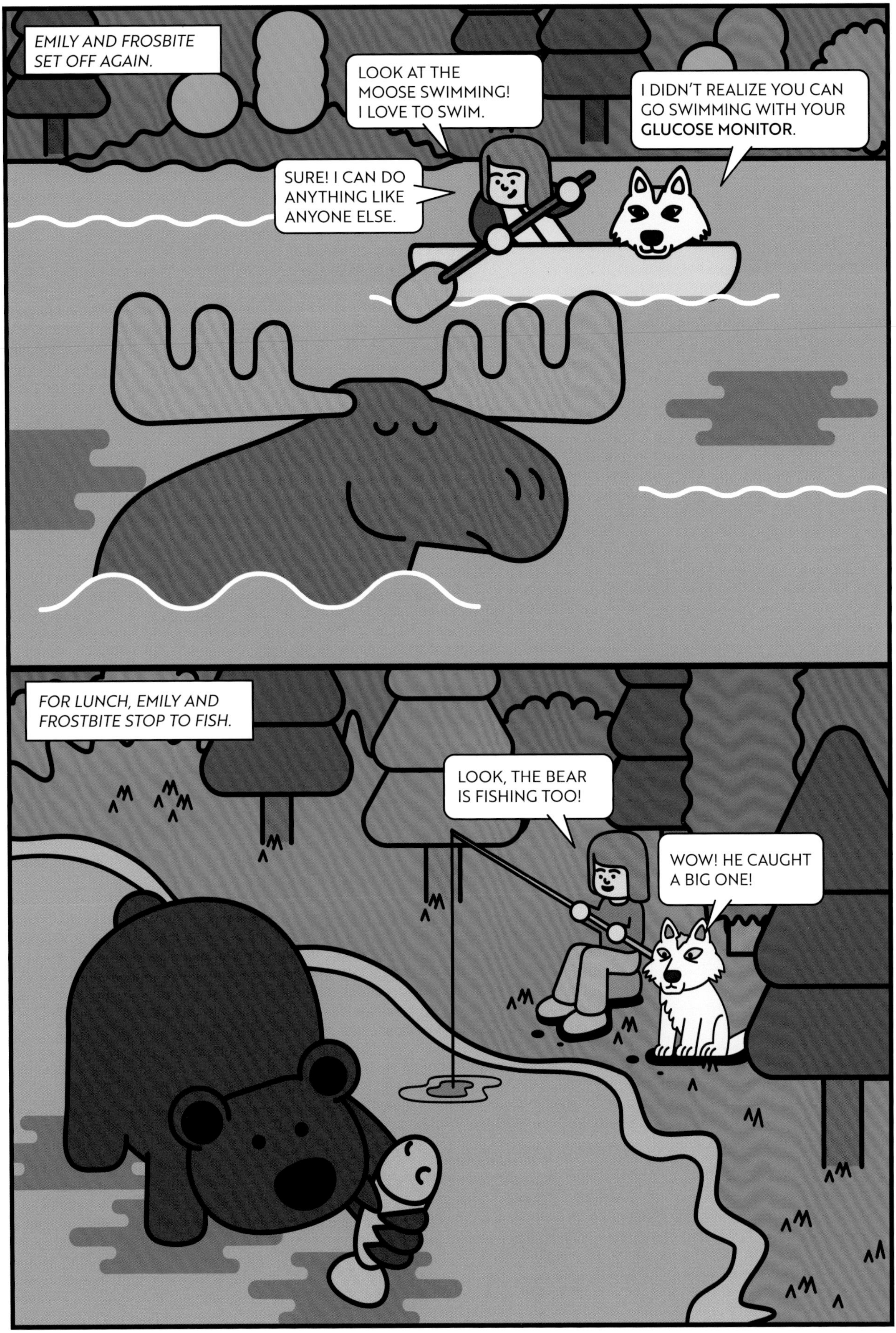
EMILY AND FROSBITE SET OFF AGAIN.
LOOK AT THE MOOSE SWIMMING! I LOVE TO SWIM.
I DIDN'T REALIZE YOU CAN GO SWIMMING WITH YOUR **GLUCOSE MONITOR**.
SURE! I CAN DO ANYTHING LIKE ANYONE ELSE.
FOR LUNCH, EMILY AND FROSTBITE STOP TO FISH.
LOOK, THE BEAR IS FISHING TOO!
WOW! HE CAUGHT A BIG ONE!

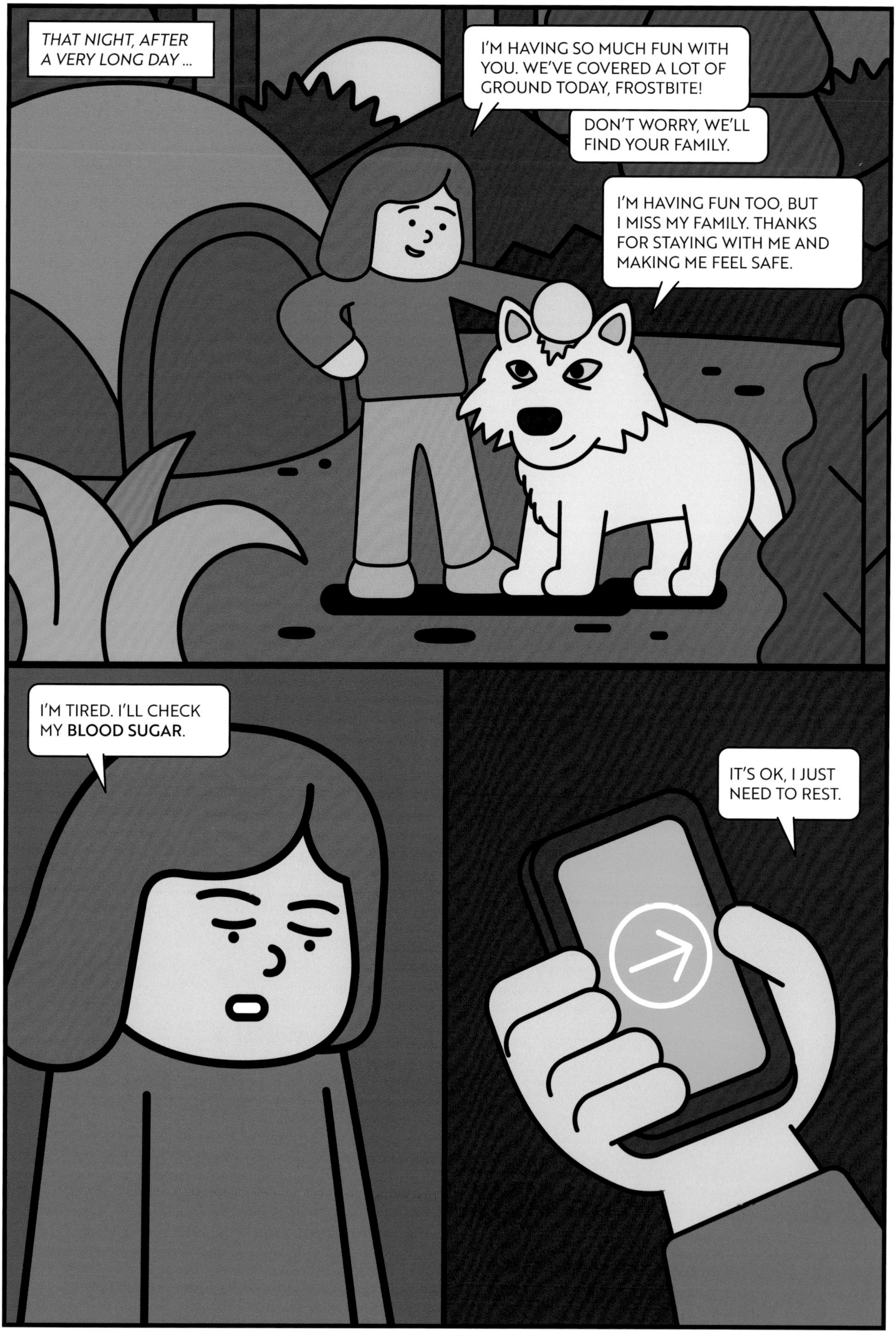
THAT NIGHT, AFTER A VERY LONG DAY ...
I'M HAVING SO MUCH FUN WITH YOU. WE'VE COVERED A LOT OF GROUND TODAY, FROSTBITE!
DON'T WORRY, WE'LL FIND YOUR FAMILY.
I'M HAVING FUN TOO, BUT I MISS MY FAMILY. THANKS FOR STAYING WITH ME AND MAKING ME FEEL SAFE.
I'M TIRED. I'LL CHECK MY **BLOOD SUGAR**.
IT'S OK, I JUST NEED TO REST.

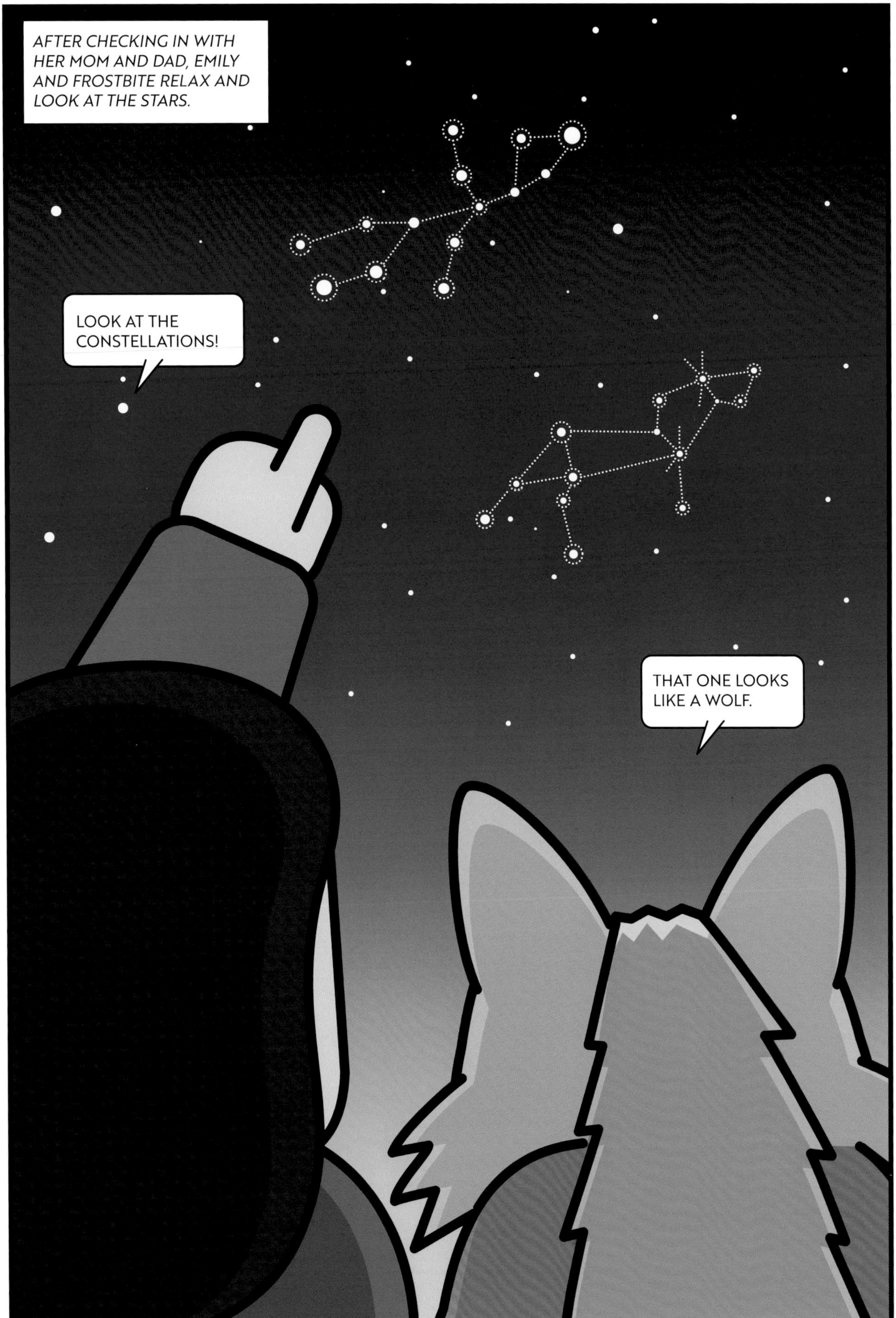
AFTER CHECKING IN WITH HER MOM AND DAD, EMILY AND FROSTBITE RELAX AND LOOK AT THE STARS.
LOOK AT THE CONSTELLATIONS!
THAT ONE LOOKS LIKE A WOLF.

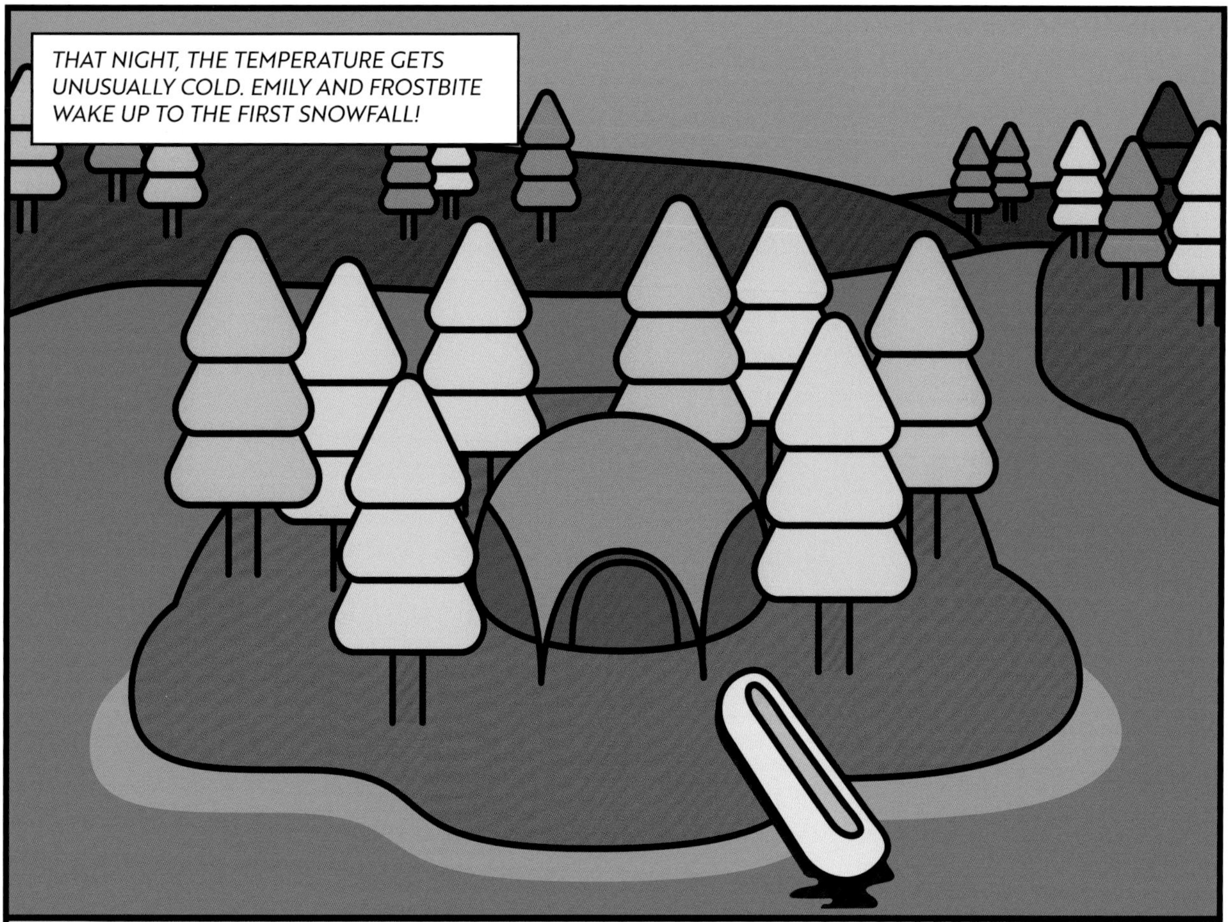
THAT NIGHT, THE TEMPERATURE GETS UNUSUALLY COLD. EMILY AND FROSTBITE WAKE UP TO THE FIRST SNOWFALL!

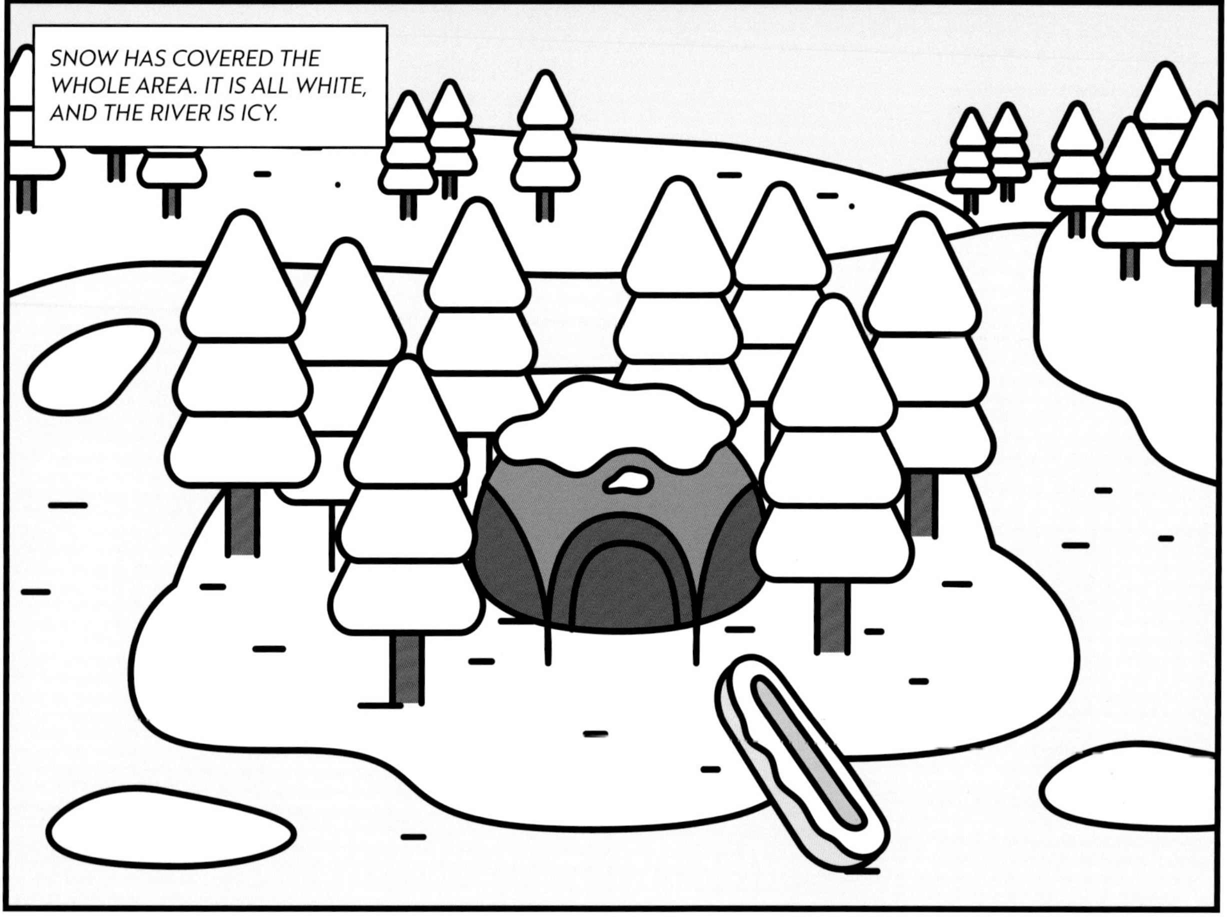
SNOW HAS COVERED THE WHOLE AREA. IT IS ALL WHITE, AND THE RIVER IS ICY.

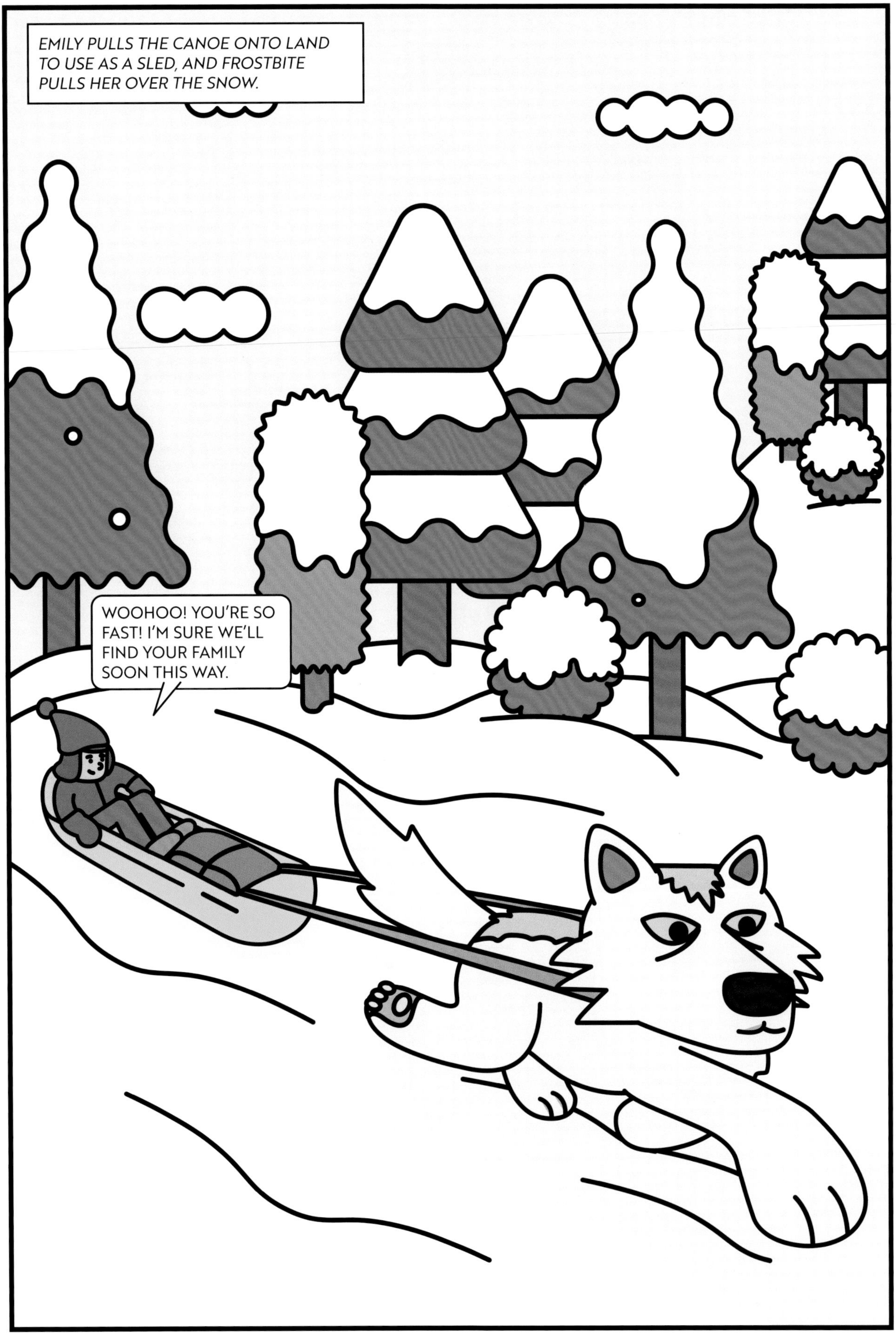
EMILY PULLS THE CANOE ONTO LAND TO USE AS A SLED, AND FROSTBITE PULLS HER OVER THE SNOW.
WOOHOO! YOU'RE SO FAST! I'M SURE WE'LL FIND YOUR FAMILY SOON THIS WAY.

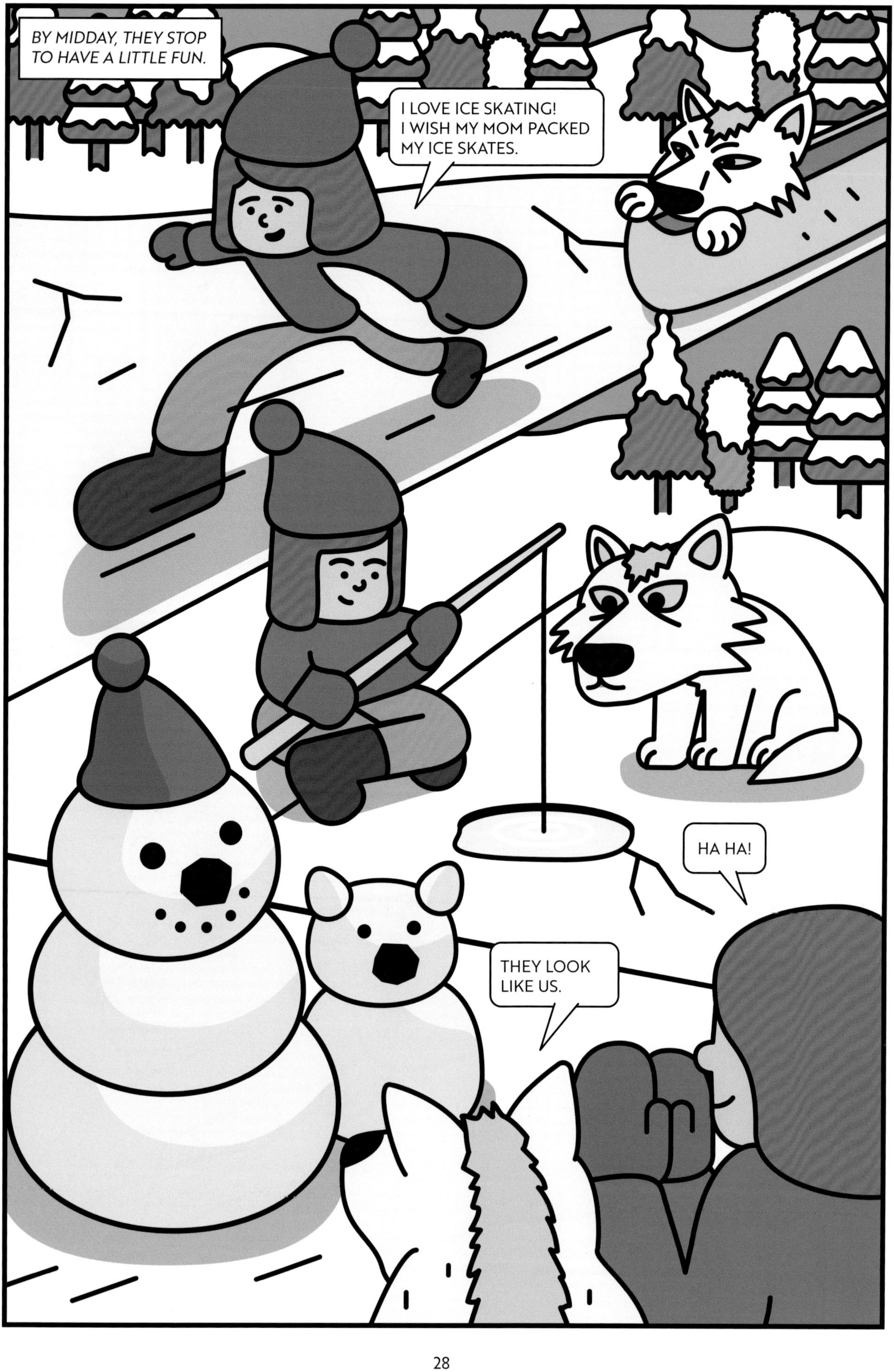
BY MIDDAY, THEY STOP TO HAVE A LITTLE FUN.
I LOVE ICE SKATING! I WISH MY MOM PACKED MY ICE SKATES.
HA HA!
THEY LOOK LIKE US.

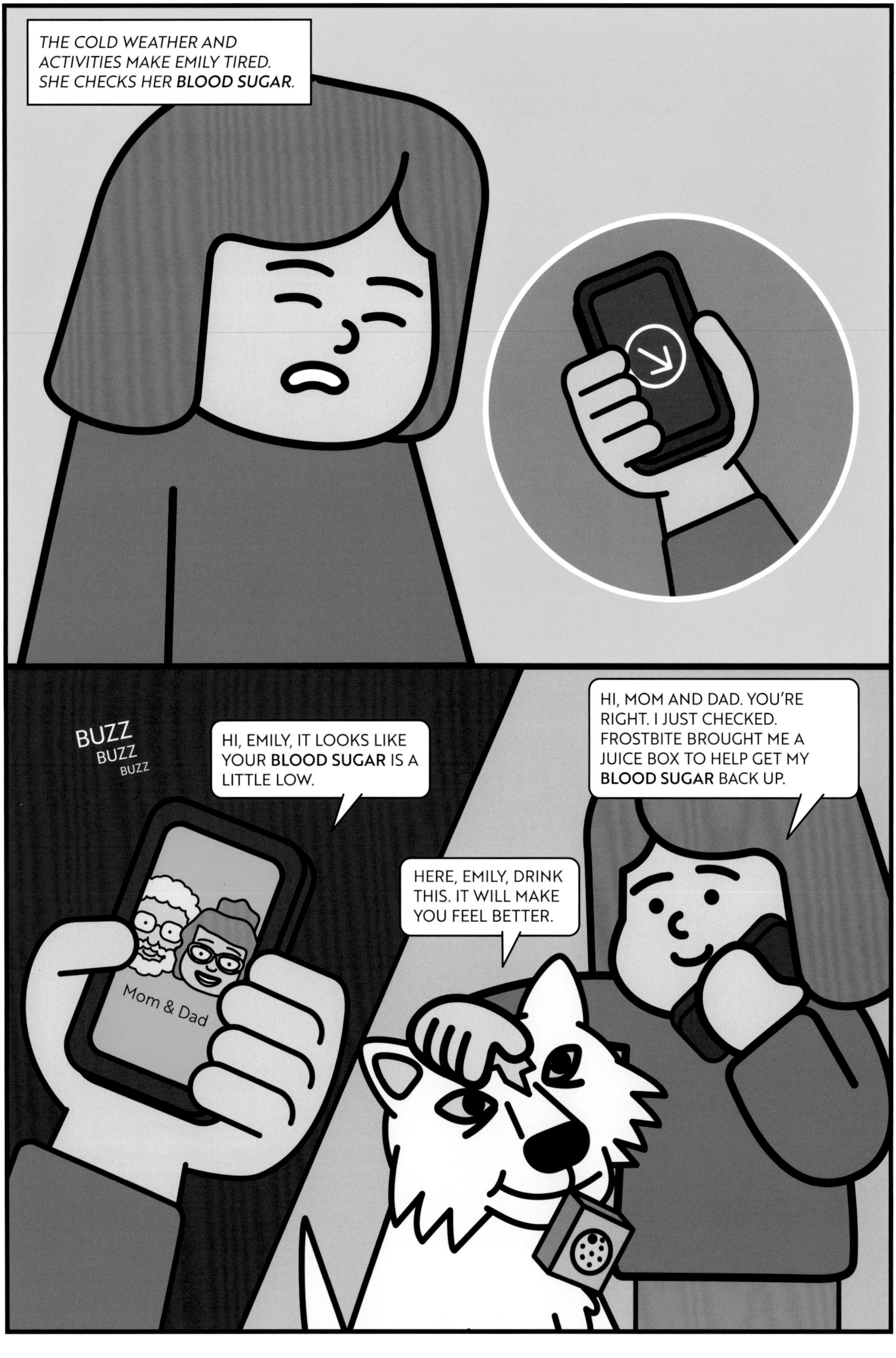
THE COLD WEATHER AND ACTIVITIES MAKE EMILY TIRED. SHE CHECKS HER **BLOOD SUGAR**.
BUZZ BUZZ BUZZ
HI, EMILY, IT LOOKS LIKE YOUR **BLOOD SUGAR** IS A LITTLE LOW.
Mom & Dad
HI, MOM AND DAD. YOU'RE RIGHT. I JUST CHECKED. FROSTBITE BROUGHT ME A JUICE BOX TO HELP GET MY **BLOOD SUGAR** BACK UP.
HERE, EMILY, DRINK THIS. IT WILL MAKE YOU FEEL BETTER.

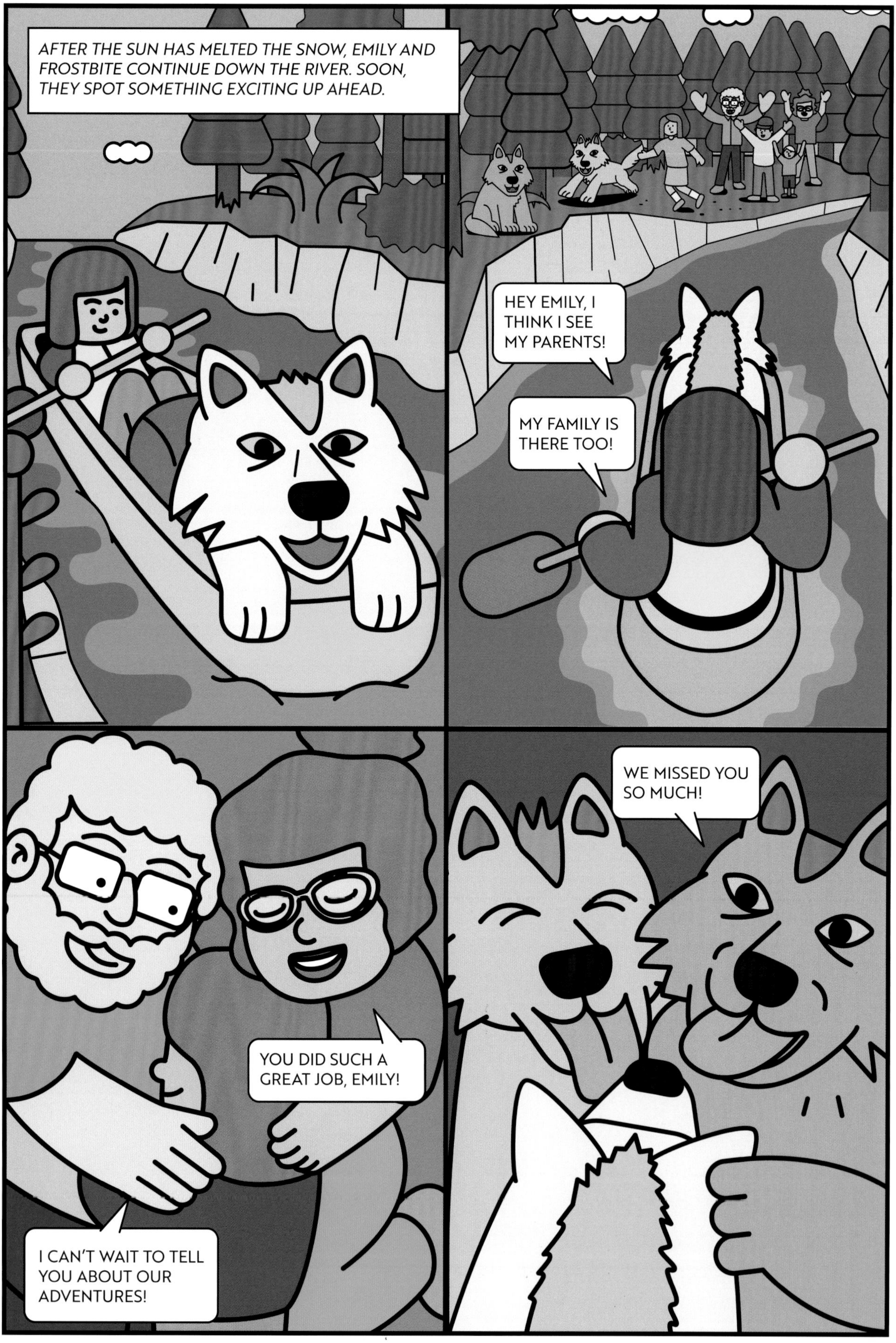

AFTER THE SUN HAS MELTED THE SNOW, EMILY AND FROSTBITE CONTINUE DOWN THE RIVER. SOON, THEY SPOT SOMETHING EXCITING UP AHEAD.
HEY EMILY, I THINK I SEE MY PARENTS!
MY FAMILY IS THERE TOO!
YOU DID SUCH A GREAT JOB, EMILY!
I CAN'T WAIT TO TELL YOU ABOUT OUR ADVENTURES!
WE MISSED YOU SO MUCH!

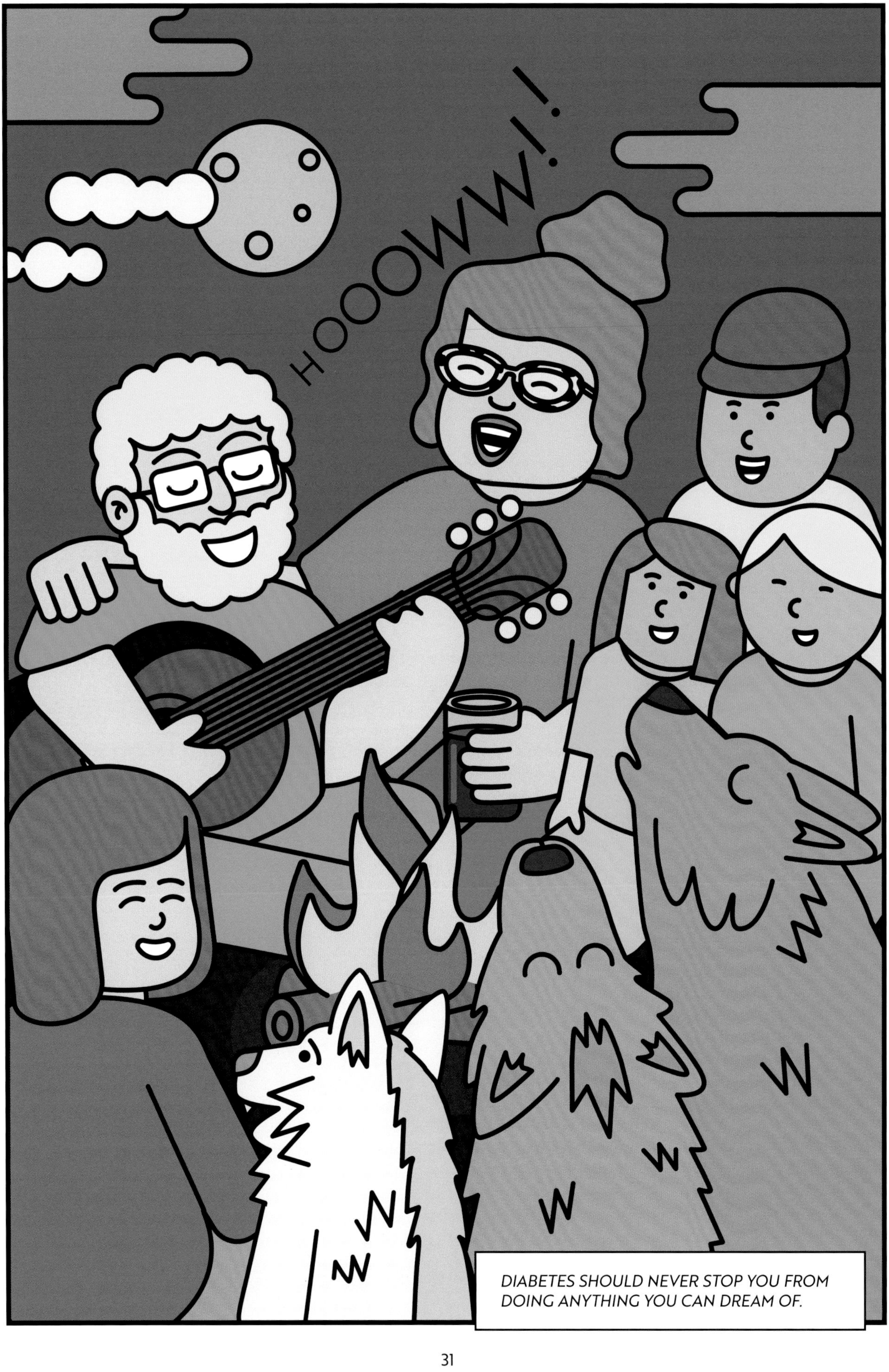
HOOOWW!!!
DIABETES SHOULD NEVER STOP YOU FROM DOING ANYTHING YOU CAN DREAM OF.

KEY TERMS

blood sugar: the concentration of a form of sugar (glucose) in the blood stream

carbohydrate: starches, sugars, and dietary fibers that come mostly from grains, fruits, vegetables and dairy products. Carbohydrates are one of the key nutrients the body needs to have energy and be healthy.

glucose monitor: a device that measures blood sugar. It is sometimes called a glucose meter.

hypoglycemia: low blood sugar

hyperglycemia: high blood sugar

insulin: a chemical (hormone) made by the pancreas that regulates the amount of sugar in the blood

pancreas: an organ that makes many hormones and enzymes to help digestion and regulate nutrients in the body. It sits behind the stomach in the belly.

MORE INFORMATION FROM THE MEDICAL EDITOR

By Ana L. Creo, M.D.
Consultant, Division of Pediatric Endocrinology and Metabolism, Mayo Clinic, Rochester, MN;
Assistant Professor of Pediatrics, Mayo Clinic College of Medicine and Science

Diabetes is a common condition in which the body doesn't process sugar well enough. It affects 10 to 20 out of 100,000 children, and more children are being diagnosed every year. People can have one of two forms of diabetes: type 1 and type 2.

Diabetes results when there's not enough **insulin**, a chemical that helps sugar enter the body's cells from the bloodstream. In type 1 diabetes, the body makes little or no **insulin**. This happens because of an autoimmune attack on the pancreas. The immune system mistakenly attacks the body's own cells. Having type 1 diabetes is often bad luck or triggered by viruses in people with an underlying genetic tendency to develop type 1 diabetes and other autoimmune conditions. Type 2 diabetes results when the **pancreas** makes **insulin**, but not enough to work well. Type 2 diabetes more commonly occurs in adolescents and adults but can sometimes affect children. This typically occurs in adolescents with a high body weight. The exact cause isn't known. But family history, genetics, diet, activity and weight may play a role.

The treatments for type 1 and type 2 diabetes are often different. Children with type 1 diabetes will always need to take **insulin**. Some children and teenagers with type 2 diabetes can take medicine to make their own **insulin** work better. All people with diabetes need to monitor their **blood sugar**, especially if they take **insulin**. There are many different devices available that help monitor a child's **blood sugar**. Some people prick their finger to check **blood sugar** while others wear a continuous **glucose monitor**, which stays on the body anywhere from 5 to 14 days. It is also important that children take the right amount of **insulin** to match what their bodies need and how much food they plan to eat. Not having enough **insulin** can result in high **blood sugar**. This can cause children to feel unwell, feel very thirsty, urinate more often, have difficulty focusing in school and can lead to long-term health problems. Likewise, taking too much **insulin** or being very active can result in low **blood sugar**. Low **blood sugar** may cause the child to be pale, sweaty, shaky or hungry, though some children don't experience any symptoms from low **blood sugar**.

While people with diabetes can sometimes have special treats, it is important that they follow a meal plan from their health care team. Eating the right kind of food and taking the right amount of **insulin** helps keep **blood sugar** in range. Keeping **blood sugar** in range helps reduce long-term complications. However, many children with diabetes still have some high and low **blood sugar** readings, and this is normal.

Newer technology and devices are making it easier for children to keep their **blood sugar** in range. For children who are managing diabetes, the long-term outlook is excellent.

REFERENCES

DiMeglio LA, Evans-Molina C, Oram RA. Type 1 diabetes. The Lancet. 2018; doi:10.1016/S0140-6736(18)31320-5.

Koren D, Levitsky LL. Type 2 diabetes mellitus in childhood and adolescence. Pediatrics in Review. 2021; doi:10.1542/pir.2019-0236.

Powers AC. Type 1 diabetes mellitus: much progress, many opportunities. Journal of Clinical Investigation. 2021; doi: 10.1172/JCI142242.

WEB RESOURCES

The American Diabetes Association — www.diabetes.org
The American Diabetes Association (ADA) works to improve the health of people with diabetes, providing information and tools, funding research and delivering services. The organization also gives a voice to those denied their rights because of diabetes. Visit their website for more information on ADA's mission and resources, education and advocacy.

The Juvenile Diabetes Research Foundation — www.jdrf.org
The Juvenile Diabetes Research Foundation (JDRF) is a nonprofit organization that provides services, advocacy and funding to support diabetes research and treatments. Visit the JDRF website to learn about daily life with type 1 diabetes, symptoms, managing it and more.

ABOUT THE MEDICAL EDITOR

Ana L. Creo, M.D.
Consultant, Division of Pediatric Endocrinology and Metabolism,
Mayo Clinic, Rochester, MN; Assistant Professor of Pediatrics, Mayo Clinic College of Medicine and Science

Dr. Creo leads the Pediatric Diabetes Center at Mayo Clinic and enjoys working with the diabetes team to help children of all ages adapt to life with diabetes. She has a special interest in diabetes technology and artificial intelligence and has published over 30 peer-reviewed articles and book chapters. Her research has been supported by institutional and external funding sources. She also has a passion for teaching trainees at all levels and has received many awards for teaching excellence.

Dr. Creo wants to acknowledge Janet Hansen, R.N., CDCES, Diabetes Educator, Division of Pediatric Endocrinology and Metabolism, Mayo Clinic, Rochester, MN, for her kind collaboration and expertise contributing to this book with her years of experience taking outstanding care of children with diabetes.

ABOUT THE AUTHORS

Guillaume Federighi, aka **Hey Gee**, is a French and American author and illustrator. He began his career in 1998 in Paris, France. He also spent a few decades exploring the world of street art and graffiti in different European capitals. After moving to New York in 2008, he worked with many companies and brands, developing a reputation in graphic design and illustration for his distinctive style of translating complex ideas into simple and timeless visual stories. He is also the owner and creative director of Hey Gee Studio, a full-service creative agency based in New York City.

Wolf Queen is the pseudonym for the Mayo Clinic patient who helped to write this book. She was diagnosed with type 1 diabetes when she was 4 years old. She was sick with what her family thought was a viral illness but then developed increased thirst and urination, and weight loss. Her parents spent several days in the hospital with her, learning how to care for her diabetes. Four years later, they are thriving. Wolf Queen still has days when her blood sugar is high or low. She and her parents do their best to manage it. Now Wolf Queen has a glucose monitor that tells her parents her blood sugar every five minutes and an insulin pump. The pump helps her automatically get the right amount of insulin.

Wolf Queen is an adventurous 8-year-old who loves to hike, swim, play basketball, practice gymnastics, fish, ride bikes, go sledding and more. She lives in Minnesota with her family and their beloved golden retriever, Teddy. When she grows up, she wants to be a park ranger that cares for wolves.

ABOUT FONDATION IPSEN BOOKLAB

Fondation Ipsen improves the lives of millions of people around the world by rethinking scientific communication. The truthful transmission of science to the public is complex because scientific information is often technical and there is a lot of inaccurate information. In 2018, Fondation Ipsen established BookLab to address this need. BookLab books come about through collaboration between scientists, doctors, artists, authors and children. In paper and electronic formats, and in several languages, BookLab delivers books across more than 50 countries for people of all ages and cultures. Fondation Ipsen BookLab's publications are free of charge to schools, libraries and people living in precarious situations. Join us! Access and share our books by visiting: www.fondation-ipsen.org.

ABOUT MAYO CLINIC PRESS

Launched in 2019, Mayo Clinic Press shines a light on the most fascinating stories in medicine and empowers individuals with the knowledge to build healthier, happier lives. From the award-winning *Mayo Clinic Health Letter* to books and media covering the scope of human health and wellness, Mayo Clinic Press publications provide readers with reliable and trusted content by some of the world's leading health care professionals. Proceeds benefit important medical research and education at Mayo Clinic. For more information about Mayo Clinic Press, visit MCPress.MayoClinic.org.

ABOUT THE COLLABORATION

The My Life Beyond series was developed in partnership between Fondation Ipsen's BookLab and Mayo Clinic, which has provided world-class medical education for more than 150 years. This collaboration aims to provide trustworthy, impactful resources for understanding childhood diseases and other problems that can affect children's well-being.

The series offers readers a holistic perspective of children's lives with — and beyond — their medical challenges. In creating these books, young people who have been Mayo Clinic patients worked together with author-illustrator Hey Gee, sharing their personal experiences. The resulting fictionalized stories authentically bring to life the patients' emotions and their inspiring responses to challenging circumstances. In addition, Mayo Clinic physicians contributed the latest medical expertise on each topic so that these stories can best help other patients, families and caregivers understand how children perceive and work through their own challenges.

Text: Hey Gee and Wolf Queen
Illustrations: Hey Gee

Medical editor: Ana L. Creo, M.D., Consultant, Division of Pediatric Endocrinology and Metabolism,
Mayo Clinic, Rochester, MN; Assistant Professor of Pediatrics, Mayo Clinic College of Medicine and Science;
in collaboration with Janet Hansen, R.N., CDCES, Diabetes Educator, Division of Pediatric Endocrinology and Metabolism, Mayo Clinic,
Rochester, MN

Managing editor: Anna Cavallo, Health Education and Content Services/Mayo Clinic Press, Mayo Clinic, Rochester, MN
Project manager: Kim Chandler, Department of Education, Mayo Clinic, Rochester, MN
Manager of publications: Céline Colombier-Maffre, Fondation Ipsen, Paris, France
President: James A. Levine, M.D., Ph.D., Professor, Fondation Ipsen, Paris, France

MAYO CLINIC PRESS
200 First St. SW
Rochester, MN 55905
mcpress.mayoclinic.org

For bulk sales to employers, member groups and health-related companies, contact Mayo Clinic, 200 First St. SW, Rochester, MN 55905, or send an email to SpecialSalesMayoBooks@mayo.edu.

Proceeds from the sale of every book benefit important medical research and education at Mayo Clinic.

ISBN 978-1-945564-16-1

Library of Congress Control Number: 2021950719

Printed in the United States of America